# 4 AM

## By: Joreen Sykes

ISBN 13: 978-0-578-14095-7
ISBN: 10: 0578140950


Printed in the United States of America
Published: May 2014

## Dedication

I dedicate this book to my two children Marcus and Nigel. Without whom my life would be uneventful. Through the good and bad, the two of you have always been the brighter side of my life. I will always continue to fight for you.

To my best friend, my soul mate, my hero, Garry. You stood by my side holding my hand and saw me through some of my darkest and loneliest moments. You have my deepest love and apprechation. Thank you for your encouragement and the sacrifices you made for me. Safe and secure is how you always make me feel. You have my love and trust that will last through multiple lifetimes. Without you at my side, I would not have made it through.

This book is also dedicated to all the parents who have lost a child and who suffer in silence. I know that a memory is not enough, and you would rather have your child here with you, but stand strong. Don't ever feel that you must accept anything that someone says to you, I encourage you to say exactly what's in your heart, even if at times it offends. YOU are the only one that knows what's in your heart, don't be afraid to speak for it, don't be afraid to speak for your child. Find love and encouragement wherever you can, your day will come.

## Acknowledgements

To my sister Dawn Locke, God-Mother to Marcus, thank you for driving from what seemed to be "in a blink of an eye" from Virginia to be at my side.

My little sister Nicole, for always helping me find my smile when you knew I was feeling down.

Franchon Beeks and Celeste Charles, my sisters, my friends, what can I say! So much about you is just the opposite of me. The strength that you possess, and being right by my side during my greatest time of need, helped to pull me through. You were there for me at a minutes notice. That showed me just how important your friendship is to me. I can thank the two of you a thousand times, and it still will never be enough.

My most heartfelt gratitude and thanks go to Sgt. Dave Spicer & Diane Glenn, of the Dover Police Department. Thank you Dave, for your unwillingness to give up on the pursuit of my son's offenders. Without your hard work, commitment, and dedication to your work, they would still be walking the streets today. Diane, as I told you before, I am just so thankful that it was you who knocked on my door that morning. The work that you do for others has been a true inspiration for me.

Thank you Kim Book, for encouraging me to start writing my journal. The support you give to me means a great deal.

There are to many of you for me to name, but I want to thank family and friends who continue to show their love of Marcus. I read each and every post you put on his Facebook page.

| | | |
|---|---|---|
| Jessica Thomas | Jamere Burris | Adrean Guy |
| Shanea Coburn | Milian Taylor | Marvin Coburn |
| Sydney Fancy | Jackie Gilmore | Shelby Williams |
| Talia Sykes | Jonathan Jenkins | Ashlyn Sykes |
| Stephanie Broschart-Burris | Jennifer Ramos | Kenya Sykes-Mickens |
| Michelle King-Sykes | Amanda & Kevin Locke | Melody Gibbs |
| Lakisha Bordley | Holly Bumbaugh | William Curtis |
| Lauren Ewing | Amber Jurney | Jody English |
| Haley Wells | Bianca Iacone | Ashley Clark |
| Rhoshadra Ransom | Janae Deshields | |

And the list goes on!

## Why I'm Writing This Book

It was never my intention to write a book, however, after the murder of my son Marcus, a friend suggested that I start to journal as a way to release my anger, frustrations and work out my emotions. It became so much more. As I began to write, I found that it was away for me to talk to my son as if he was still here. To tell him how I am feeling and what I've been going through. I used it to talk to him about all that has been going on since he's been gone, particularly in regards to his case. Towards the end of the second year of me writing, I soon came to realize that there are other parents who may be experiencing the exact same things as me. So, I'm taking the words of my journal, and sharing them with you in this book.

Sharing my journal and exposing my most vulnerable moments, is at the very least, a daunting task, it's not easy. But it is my hope that my personal experience gives understanding to others as to the severity and emotional depths that a parent who has loss a child to gun violence, or any type of violence that claims a life, can go through.

I know that to many of you, my book or my style of writing might not make sense, and may seem a little all over the place, just keep in mind that I was writing from a state of confusion and from a place of anger. Many days I could not keep a straight thought in my head. Some days my emotions, my anger, and hatred would just flow through me like rushing water, and I couldn't get control over my emotions, my thoughts, or my crying. Struggling with the intense feeling I was experiencing at the exact time that I was trying to write and express my feeling to my son was extremely difficult, but I was determined to get down on paper and express my feelings to him.

But also, while creating my book, I wanted to keep the integrity of how I originally wrote to him without changing too much, but making it so that you could understand.

While a person's intentions may be true, sincere and meaningful, in no way do I want to speak for what someone else may be going through, "to each his own" but for me during my time of darkness, there were certain things that people would say or do that aggravated me. One thing I truly hated was to be coddled in public. For instance, one thing that I could not stand was to be hugged. When I would see people, or tell someone for the first time that my son had passed away, one of the first things that they wanted to do was hug. Even though I know that hugging is a way that expresses love, comfort and concern when someone is grieving, it was not something that I wanted or desired all the time. Hugging to me just makes me more emotional. Not to say that I don't hug sometimes when I see a good friend, because I do, it's just that at that time, for that reason, I didn't. I also hated for people to tell me that my son is with God, that he is in a better place, God has called him home. With all due respect, that didn't bring me comfort. I'd rather have my son home with me. People would say to me, at least you have memories, memories are not enough! Memories are not a substitute for not having him here. Some would say, you need to find closure in your heart, or you need to forgive, Really! My son is gone, how do I find closure or forgiveness in that? I think that sometimes people don't know what to say, so they say things that they "think" would be comforting to you. Unless you have personally experienced the loss of a child in this way, and so suddenly, how could you possibly know what, how or when I should be feeling something? I say....if you don't know what to say or how to say it, don't say anything at all! People need to know that sometimes, silence is grand, silence in itself is worth more than a thousand words. In a support group that I attended, they mentioned a post that someone came across, I don't know where it originated from or who wrote it, but they shared it with us, to quote a little bit:

*Please don't ask me if I'm over it yet, I'll never get over it; Please don't tell me he's in a better place, he's not here with me; Please don't say at least he isn't suffering, I haven't come to terms with why he had to suffer at all; Please don't tell me you know how I feel unless you have lost a child; Please don't ask me if I feel better, bereavement isn't a condition that clears up and goes away; Please don't tell me you had him for so many years, what year would you chose for your child to die?*

You know, I don't know who wrote that, but they hit the nail on the head with that one, it speaks volume. While I do appreciate the sympathy and concern people displayed to me, I really just wished that they would just think about what they say or what they were asking first.

There were so many challenges that I faced after the death of Marcus, or maybe I'm just being overly sensitive, who could blame me? All I know is that certain things irritated me to no end. But the biggest thing that I could not, no...let me rephrase that, the main thing that I could not stand, is to be continuously asked, "what happen!" Just saying that my son was murdered isn't enough for some people; people have a natural desire to want to know the full details. Where? How? How many times was he shot? How long did he live? Things like that pissed me off. People need to know and understand that when they ask a person "what happen" just to satisfy their own morbid curiosity, they are asking for that person to relive the most devastating moment in their life all over again, that's not cool! Some people might not mind talking about those specific details. The first year was the hardest for me, I couldn't stand that question. I wanted people to just leave me alone. But as soon as you don't give details, then they start to form judgments or opinions, and it's always on the negative side. Not to say that someone being murdered isn't negative enough, but they will first assume that the person must have been doing or been involved in something illegal, so not the case here!

Now, on the flip side of my above statements, I know that there are people who do need that attention, they want and need to talk, but don't know how to go about it, where to start or how to get help. Being verbal about their emotions is what works for them. Me being me, I chose to go through and experience my pain in my own way, in my own time, and without the influence of what society thinks I should be doing, or how I should be feeling at that point in time. I chose to suffer in silence. As you will soon read, I had very dark, emotional, and dangerous moments that not even the one person closest to me knew about. I know that sometimes being quiet about what I've gone through was not always a good idea, and this is why I've decided to share my journal with you.

It's also my hope that this book is read by young adults. I want you to stop, take a step back, and think about what you are doing before you pull that trigger to take another person's life. Think about the aftermath, not only will you be ruining your own future, your own life, think about the other person's family that you will be destroying. Better yet, think about this, I could be your mother, sister, aunt, or grandmother that's suffering. It could be YOU, that's lying in a casket 6 feet underground covered with dirt. I could be your mother writing this book, pleading for the senseless crimes to end.

I wish that you would just take some time, just take a minute to search your soul and ask yourself "is what I'm about to do, is this truly something worth killing or dying over? An argument, a fist fight, someone had beef with my boy that I really had nothing to do with, or someone stepped to my girl, or some damn hear-say?" Is any of that really worth putting my family through the pain, shame and embarrassment over?" I say hell no! An argument... it's just words! A fist fight...now that's how MEN handle it! Over a girl, get another! Hear-say...someone is always going to add their own twist to the story anyway, so you don't know what the truth is anyway. How petty can you be to want to fight or kill over some bullshit like that?

And what if you already have your own kids, is this what you would really want for them? Is this the life style you would want them to have? Most parents want more for their children then what they had themselves. Do you think that your parents wanted this for you?

You know what gets me, y'all young kids be out there running the streets, robbing, stealing, shooting, selling drugs, and hurting people like you don't have a care in world. But as soon as you get caught and go to jail (because eventually you will get caught), now all of a sudden you want pity, you want forgiveness, or now you found Jesus and you changed your life around. Well, you should have been looking for Jesus before you committed that crime! Because there's no coming back from death!

I say all this to say that the acts and the decisions you make affect more than just one person, there are many, many layers in a person's life that is affected. And Why, why would you want to live your days constantly looking over your shoulder? Running from the law, wondering if someone is coming after you, wondering if someone is going to cap you while you're walking down the street, wondering if the police is going to roll up on you or raid your home in the middle of the night? Is all that stress really worth putting your family and loved ones through? Damn!

My younger son Nigel must now live without his big brother, without the one person who always had his back, the one that he loved and shared a life with for 22 years. And now, Nigel must now resolve to being an only child. And me.... I have a void in my heart for my son that is so huge.....and I don't know how to fill it.

# Introduction

## Marcus LeJon Ware

In the early morning hours on October 8, 2011, the most horrific, and traumatic event changed my life forever. At 4 a.m. I received a knock on my door, my son Marcus had just been shot and didn't make it. The events of that night continue to play over-and-over in my head, and haunts me to this very day.

He was born Marcus LeJon Ware on March 9, 1989, believe me when I tell you, he took my breath away. He was the most handsome baby I had ever seen, but why wouldn't he, he's my son. I would have to say, that was my first of many profound moments in life, and I wouldn't change a thing.

Like many mothers, adjusting to motherhood for this first time, it was challenging, but Marcus made it easy. Marcus didn't give me any real headaches as a child or teen, at least no more than the typical teenager. Marcus had always been reserved and to himself, unless he knew you, and he always had a smile on his face. His friends nick-named him Smiley. The very first tattoo of many, he got was of a giant smiley face on his stomach, trust me when I tell you, I was not happy about that!

Growing up, my boys were not the typical kids that played with little model race cars, toy trains, or action figures. They liked to play with live animals and bring them in the house; snakes; frogs, and bugs. They both liked to go fishing, Nigel more so than Marcus. I remember when Marcus was 11, he was bitten by a bat that he was trying to rescue.

# Rabid bat attacks child in Dover

**By Michele Shock**
Staff writer

DOVER — A child has learned the hard way about not playing with wild animals.

Marcus Ware, 11, of Dover was playing at his cousin's house in the 800 block of Towne Point in Dover Friday afternoon when he was bit by a rabid bat.

"He saw the bat laying on the ground in the yard and picked it up to play with it," said Marcus' mother, Joreen Sykes.

"When he went to put the bat back down, that is when he got bit."

Ms. Sykes said she wanted to make sure they caught the bat, so it could be tested for rabies.

According to Murray Goldthwaite, director of the Kent County SPCA, the test came back positive.

On Wednesday, members of Dover's Animal Control Service, the SPCA and Wildlife Management Services LLC of Lincoln came to the house where the rabid bat had been nesting.

The bats were found on the side of the house, near the chimney and are believed to still be in the rafters, Mr. Goldthwaite said.

He said the officials were there to catch the rest of the bats in the colony so they could be tested, too.

A trap was set on the side of the house to catch the remaining bats.

"We have sealed the area where the colony is and have attached a large tube to where their opening is," he said.

"The bats should follow down the tube and go into the trap and they cannot back out."

Carson L. Kennard, a consultant with Wildlife Management Services, said the trap could hold 100 to 150 bats.

Mr. Goldthwaite said the bats will be euthanized and then tested for rabies.

Ms. Sykes said Marcus started his rabies shots on Tuesday.

"He got three shots on Tuesday and he will have to get a five-shot series, which will have to be completed within a month's time."

"It didn't surprise me that he picked the bat up," she said. "He plays with different animals all the time and collects all kinds, such as snakes and crabs and keeps them in our shed."

Marcus said he wanted to pick up the bat because it looked hurt.

"After I picked the bat up it started screeching," he said. "It didn't scare me because it was such a low noise.

"After it started screeching, I went to go put it on a tree, it bit me and then when I tried putting it down it bit really hard on my thumb.

"When I finally got it on the ground, and when the bat hopped out of my hand it bit my thumb again."

*Michele Shock can be reached at 741-8225 or micheles@newszap.com.*

Marcus had a protective nature, for his brother, but also for his closest friends. I recall when he was in 9th or 10th grade, he got into a fight with another student. There was a student, another young boy that was picking and teasing on a young girl in school, Marcus did not know either of these people, but felt that he had to come to the defence of the young girl, which ultimately lead to the fight. The school of course called me because Marcus had been suspended for fighting, but you know what, I couldn't be mad with him. Yes, I know fighting is fighting and its wrong, but to take a stand and defend someone who could not defend themselves is commendable! Who could be mad at that? Marcus was pretty much this way all throughout his life.

Marcus later went on to attend Job Corp in Potomac, Maryland, just outside of Washington DC. I can't remember the full details but the course he wanted to take he couldn't because he had to be 18, he was only 17 at the time. I think the course had something to do with law enforcement, so he chose brick masonry instead. I told him over and over to really think about if that was what he wanted to do. Me knowing him, I didn't think he would like it too much, but he excelled in the program anyway.

He graduated not only at the TOP of his class but 4 months early as well. One of his instructors called me to tell me how impressed he was with Marcus, and how he had so much potential. All of his instructors gave him wonderful letters of recommendation.

Less than a year after coming home from Job Corp, he got a job with Forman Industries as an installer, where he continued to work for 3 ½ years. At the time of his death, he was off work on workmen's compensation from falling about 15 to 18ft from the top of a scaffold. He banged up his shoulder pretty good and his foot.

People have questioned as to why Marcus was in Dover at all the night of his death, being that we lived in Wilmington DE at the time. The answer....because to him, Dover was home. Both my children were born and raised in Dover, I myself also grew up in Dover. When we moved to Wilmington in 2005, my kids were for the most part.....in the early teens. Marcus didn't really want to go to Wilmington, Nigel on the hand, well he's for whatever. Marcus is like a rooted tree, where Nigel is like flowing water. So when Marcus got his car, he would always drive back and forth to Dover on the weekends when he was home from work to be with his friends. His job kept him away Monday through Friday. He would go to different states and work; he got to see a lot of different states. So he would stay with is Aunt Nicole whenever he would go to Dover.

Marcus was very well liked, always the jokester. Every time I think about my son, I cry, his life was so promising. Not to sound cliché, but to know him, is to love him. I could go on-and-on about the joys my boys brought to my life, but the end result now is that my younger son is without his big brother.

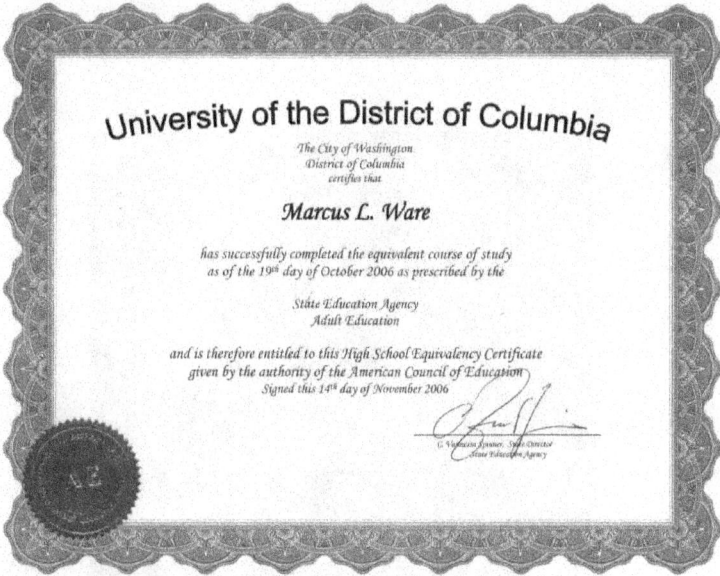

University of the District of Columbia

The City of Washington
District of Columbia
certifies that

*Marcus L. Ware*

has successfully completed the equivalent course of study
as of the 19th day of October 2006 as prescribed by the

State Education Agency
Adult Education

and is therefore entitled to this High School Equivalency Certificate
given by the authority of the American Council of Education
Signed this 14th day of November 2006

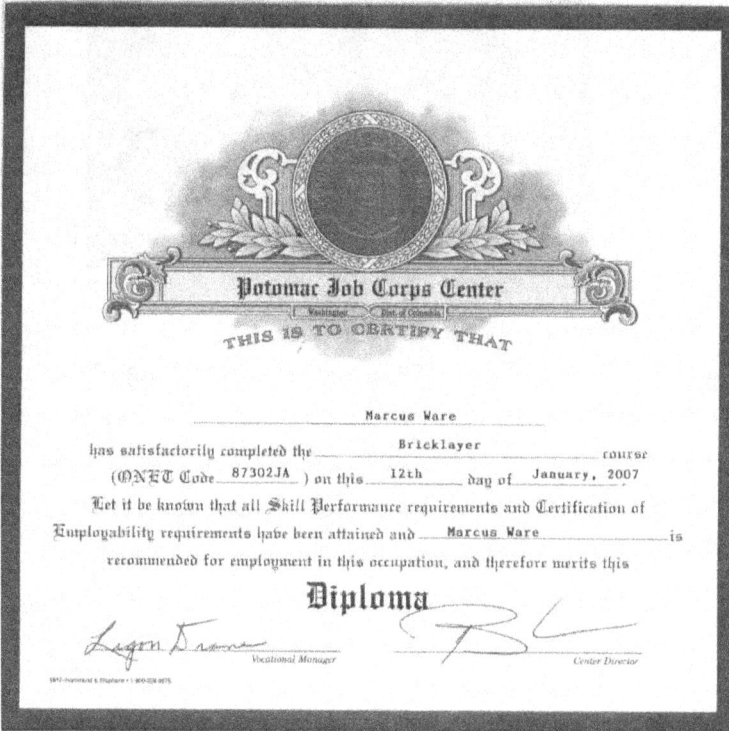

Potomac Job Corps Center

THIS IS TO CERTIFY THAT

Marcus Ware

has satisfactorily completed the _____ Bricklayer _____ course
(ONET Code ___87302JA___ ) on this ___12th___ day of ___January, 2007___

Let it be known that all Skill Performance requirements and Certification of
Employability requirements have been attained and ___Marcus Ware___ is
recommended for employment in this occupation, and therefore merits this

## Diploma

Vocational Manager                    Center Director

Marcus LeJon Ware
March 9, 1989 - October 8, 2011

## Friday, October 28, 2011 @ 3:15 PM

Marcus, they got 'em, they got 'em!! I can't believe it, they got 'em! They arrested 3 guys, Lionel Williamson, Warren Brooks, and Kurt Dupree, they got them! They said that there was a fourth person in the car who hasn't been identified yet, but they got them 3 bastards!

My heart is beating so fast right now, I can't stand it! I don't know how or when it happened, but at this point Marc, who cares. I do know that Kurt Dupree was arrested or charged in Maryland, or he was in jail in Maryland or something. But they just called me, to tell me that all three have been charged in your case. I didn't think that it was going to happen this fast, but I'm glad that it did!

My mind is so all over the place right now, I'm shaking, I am trying to take this all in. As far as I can recall, Kurt Dupree was being detained in a jail in Maryland, I don't know why, but I think that it was in MD where he was first questioned by Det. Spicer. I don't remember where or how the other 2 were captured. I'm sure that they told me, but I just have so much running in my mind I'm don't think I took it all in. But if I remember I'll tell you.


## Tuesday, November 1, 2011 at 6:20 PM

Hi Marcus, I see now that I hate coming to you like this. This should not have happened, not to you! You had so much going for you....so much. Who are these guys? Why did they do this? Marcus these past few weeks for me have been a whirl-wind. My mind won't stop spinning. I can't sleep at night. I went to Dr. O's office because I just can't get any sleep, if I am sleeping, it doesn't feel like it. He gave me a prescription for Xanax. Marcus they're not working. I have been waking up somewhat around about the same hour that you were killed, or about the time when they came to my door around 4:00 AM to give me the news. I don't know why, I just keep waking up. Even when I take the Xanax, I still wake up, I take 2 pills at once, I still wake up. I'm so tired! I don't know what to do. My body hurts so much. I want to take this whole bottle. I wish I could touch you, I just want to touch your skin, I want to see you, I want to make sure that you're ok, just to see you, that's all! I need to know that you're ok. Marc, my hands sting, my breast hurt, my chest hurts, my legs! My legs, sometimes I can't even feel them. I went to Dover the other day, and I can't remember the drive. I mean I know I got up that morning, but the next thing I knew, I was in Dover. Marcus, I just don't know what I am going to do, I want to be with you, to see you and talk to you. OMG Marcus I want so badly just to touch you right now. Marcus my hands are shaking so bad right now, I can hardly write.

## Wednesday, November 2, 2011 @ 1:45 AM

Marcus this is what I have so far. You had went to Frightland with Jamere Friday night and afterwards you had went to a party in Camden at somebody's house after you had dropped Jamere off at home, but you had gotten there late assumingly, because you were not able to get in, this is what Jessica tells me. She said that you came to the party by yourself. She was talking to you outside of the party, at one point you were standing by your car by yourself, but Jessica could see you from where she was standing, she said that someone walked over to you and said something to you. She said that by the look on your face, she felt that something was wrong, or just didn't look right. After he walked away, she walked over to you and asked you who that was, you said that you didn't know, but he had either asked you for a light or a smoke. She said that before she walked over to you, she could tell from the look on your face that you didn't know who the guy was.  She felt that if you had known the guy that you would have given him some dap or had a conversation with him or something. Jessica was riding with her friends, but she said that you wanted y'all to go to your Aunt Nikki's house to play Wii, but she was tired and had to go to work in the morning. She said that y'all left the party around about the same time. So basically as far as I am concerned, she was the last one of your close friends to see you alive that night.

I'm told that at the Sunoco gas station, you were parked there for about 20 minutes, because your car had broken down, your car battery died. Now I'm told that this gas station is a typical hang out for young people, especially after parties. So I'm assuming that this is why you were there, and knowing you, you were sitting there playing/blasting your music in your car with the engine off....and this is why your battery died. Sgt. Spicer tells me that your car was parked on the North end of the gas station facing McDonald's. What I am not clear about is how long you were there before the boys in the car drove up and parked on the South end of the gas station, facing the Home Depot. Sgt. Spicer said it looked like 4 individuals in the car, but only 3 got out, or they all got out but he could only see 3, Warren Brooks, Kurt Dupree and Lionel Williamson. I can't remember all the details he told me about who went where once they got out of the car but I vaguely remember him saying Warren Brooks went into the store to use the bathroom, but couldn't so he came back out. He then started talking to some girl outside. Now check this out Marcus, the girl he was talking to was actually parked right next to you. I don't know if he already knew this girl or what, but I'm told that they exchanged cell phone numbers. When Kurt Dupree got out of the car, I think he said that he was standing near the doors of the store. I don't recall where Lionel Williams was. Anyway, they all got back in the car and just sat there for a few minutes. Then Lionel Williamson gets out of the car, goes behind the gas station, and then a few seconds later he went back to the car. He gets out the car again, goes back behind the gas station, reappears from behind the gas station on the North side, where you are, and shoots you. But let me back up Marc, at the same time that all of this is going on, Warren Brooks is still standing in front the gas station, I'm told that he calls the girl that he was just talking to, that he got the phone number from, the girl that was parked right next to you, he calls her and tells her that she needs to get out of there because something is about to happen, and sure enough, she moves her car. Also at this same time, somebody you knew was about to help you. They were moving their car around and getting it situated so that they could give you a jump. But Lionel Williamson comes from behind the building and shoots you 4 times in the back just as you were leaning over. I guess you had or was just about to pop the hood open on your car so that person could give you a jump. You didn't even see it coming Marcus, in the back......how cowardly is that? 4 times Marcus, why would he want to do this to you? Afterwards, Lionel Williamson runs back behind the gas station towards the Home Depot, and Kurt Dupree who was driving the car, drives towards Home Depot with the car lights off, to go find Lionel Williamson. They had this planned Marcus, why else would Warren

Brooks warn that girl to move because something was about to happen and why would Kurt Dupree drive with the lights off? All I know Marc, is that they took your life, and for what? I want to know? I wish I could go to the prison right now and ask them why? Just Why?

## Thursday, November 3, 2011 @ 10:20 PM

Marcus, I can't believe that this is us. I can't believe that this has happened to our family. I just keep crying the words "my son, my son" over and over! Why? Not you! When I think about it, I can't breathe, I feel like there is a ton of brick sitting on my chest. I get this lump in my throat and I can't swallow, hot flashes, it just doesn't stop! I want to tell you about the different emotions I've been having but I can't. I want to tell you so much, but I just get so overcome with tears. I never thought that this would happen to you. I mean, I never worried about you, I always knew that whatever you did at the end of the day, you would do the right thing. I'm not saying that I knew your every move, and I know that you might have been out there doing things that I would not have approved of, and I in no way want people to think, that I think that my children walk on water, but all I have to go by is how I know you, the type of person that I know you to be. You've never been to jail, you weren't on drugs, you worked, you had your own car and money, you always had a pretty girlfriend, you finished school, you were smart and you are protective. What was there for me to worry about? From all of the friends that I know that you have, they all seem to be good people. I like them all, you know I always say that Jamere is my adopted son, and I always said that Adrian was my daughter-in-law. So I can't seem to wrap my head around WHY this happened!

I wish I could put into words how my heart aches for you. I wish you were home. My hands are stinging, my hand hurts, I just want to touch you so much. I have to constantly rub my hands together just to get them to stop. My head won't stop pounding. I don't want to get out of bed most days. Marcus, how do I make this stop?

## Saturday, November 5, 2011 @ 7:15 PM

I can't make sense of all this. People are telling me different stories about who could have and for what reason done this to you. I think that I have heard about 5 different stories now, and 2 of them seem to be over that girl Emily you were seeing. I feel like I'm in a daze, I'm not really here. I am so empty inside right now.

## Friday, November 18, 2011 @ 2:45 AM

Hey Marcus, I have been talking with the police department about your case and getting updates. There's a Detective David Spicer who is in charge of your case. I was introduced to him at the police station while I was talking with Ms. Glenn. She was the person who came to the house to tell me about you, they both seem like very nice people. I'm just feeling out of place about all this. I mean, it's weird because I feel like when I am in front of people, that I'm not acting the right way. You know how you see people on TV falling all out, screaming and hollering, being consoled by several different people. That's not me, I'm not acting like that, I know that I shouldn't, but I feel embarrassed about all of this. I know that I shouldn't, you're my son, and I'm supposed to show what ever feelings I may be having. But, I'm not comfortable with people seeing me like this. I would rather be at home ALONE when I know that I can't pull it together. Marcus, am I wrong for that? It doesn't mean that I don't love you any less or anything like that, but you know how I am about my privacy. Besides I don't want people thinking that there is something wrong with me. I'd rather cry at home, alone, and it's not that I think that people who act or carry on in that manner is wrong, or being overly dramatic, you express your pain the way that your body releases it. That's just not me, I don't think it's me, I won't allow that to be me. I'll keep it in. Who knows, maybe I'll have my breaking moment. But now that I think about it, maybe I did have my moment at the funeral. I don't remember much of it. I remember pulling the cloth over your face and I remember a little bit of the repast, that's about it!

## Tuesday, December 6, 2011 @ 12:45 AM

I can't do this Marcus, it hurts to much to go through this. I feel so alone. I feel like I have no one. Nothing is going right, no one will answer my questions, and I have so many questions. I want to know so much about what happen to you. Why someone would want to hurt you; who or what people tried to help you that night; did you call for me; did you know what had just happened to you; I want to know who all is being questioned. I just have so many things going through my head, it's like I can't keep a single straight thought for more than a minute before something else comes to mind. I feel like my mind is racing, my heart, my chest always feels heavy, like someone is sitting on me. I'm just so tired, but my body won't let me sleep. I mean I know that I'm sleeping, it just doesn't feel like it. I just want to close my eyes and not wake up. I want to forget that this is happening and this is all just a dream. I can't go through the day without crying.

I went to a group support meeting tonight for the first time here in Wilmington, Marcus I will never go there again! I will never go to that support group again! Marcus I understood that before I went there, that if I didn't want to talk that I didn't have to, I could just sit and listen if I wanted to. I got a phone call from I guess the facilitator of the group last week, she mailed me some information about the group, the directions, and some other things like that. It clearly said that I Do Not have to talk, but they ask that I respect the privacy of others that are there. Everyone in the room went around and introduced themselves and told what circumstances brought them there. The whole time, I just sat there with my head down and cried, so why, why Marcus when it got to be my turn to introduce myself, I clearly didn't want or was ready to talk. But all they did was just sit there and stare at me, the whole room was quiet, it felt like a whole 10 minutes went by for them waiting for me to talk. Marcus I felt so pressured. Then someone said to me, "Ok Joreen what brings you here tonight, can you tell us what happen to your son." Marcus I thought we didn't have to talk. I started crying even more, I sat there and just shook my head no because I didn't want to talk. But again she asks me, "What happen to your son?" So after about another "what seemed like another 5 minutes" of me just sitting there crying even harder I said what happen to you. So after I said everything, everybody just sat there and stared at me. Nobody said anything. It was just the stares that I got that made me feel like they were being judgmental. I could just see in their faces that they were thinking that you must have been doing something illegal like drugs, gang banging, robbing a store or something like that. Even though they didn't say it, or ask it, I could just see it in their faces. Marcus, I got so angry. I felt like the way that they were looking at me, made me feel like I had to defend you. So I felt obligated to tell a little more about the conditions of how you died. About how your car wouldn't start, because of the battery, that basically you were in the right place and the wrong time. Marcus I should not have had to go through that, that wasn't right!  Marcus, you should have seen how they were looking at me. I was the only parent there whose child was murdered. Everyone else was there because either their child took their own life or in a car accident, and I'm almost pretty sure that one other's sister was ill. No one, I mean no one was there in my situation. I know a life gone is still an emotional thing no matter how they left this earth, but my pain is different. With the people whose child committed suicide, they said that their kids showed signs that they were struggling with drug addictions or emotional problems. Marcus, you were suddenly taken from me, with no warnings! How can any of them relate to that? And to think that in about a year, I'm going to have to relive this all over again in court, while looking at the person that took you. What was I thinking about going there? What was I expecting? I can't go there again, that's all there is to that, not again! Marcus, I never had anyone make me feel this bad about what happened to you. I had to defend you! I should not have said anything in that group. I should have just got up and left. Maybe it's just too soon for me to try to go to a support group, I don't know. All I do know is that if a person can't except me saying that you "passed away," then that's just tough shit! They don't need to know all the ins-and-outs of everything that happened to you, the how, when and where. If you didn't hear about it in the paper, then oh well!

## Tuesday, December 25, 2011 @ 7:45 pm

Hey Marcus, this is the first Christmas without both you and Nigel, I am so lonely, this is so hard. I can't believe that you are gone; I can't believe that they took your life, why did you have to die? Why Marcus, why? I have been crying all day. My heart and my body hurts so bad, I wish I could express to you what this pain feels like. It's not emotional pain Marcus, my body hurts, I ache, I can barely write, my hands won't stop shaking, I want to tell you so much about what has been going on, but I can't keep a straight thought in my head, I feel like my mind in racing. I lay down and it feels like the room is moving and spinning, Im actually holding on to the bed.

Marcus I don't know what to do. No one has even called me to check up on me to see how I am doing, family or otherwise. A few of your friends called me on Thanksgiving to say hello and that they were thinking about me. A few more of your friends posted on your Facebook page that they are thinking of you. But me.... nothing, I get nothing. I am here all alone, just sitting. You know people don't know how much losing a child hurts. People are all consumed with themselves and their own families right now, can't say that I blame though, why should they go out of their way for me, for us?

## Saturday, January 7, 2012 @ 11:45 PM

Hey Marcus, as you know your grandmother, just died, and it's only been just less than 3 months since you left. I wanted to drive down to SC to be with her, but I also have your bowling fundraiser on Sunday. I know that it's my mom, but she is being cremated, but her memorial is going to be back up here in Dover. I could have drove down before she passed, but just like dad, I didn't want to watch them as they passed away. That is not the memory I want. And this is your first foundation fundraiser. I can't cancel it now, people have already signed up and paid money. I know it sounds crude, but it's not like mom's death was all-of-a sudden, she had been declining now for a while, we all knew that this day was coming soon. And it just so happen to be just before your fundraiser. Well, as you know I didn't go to SC, I'll be here for you right now, and then I'll be there for mom at her memorial.

## Tuesday, January 24, 2012 @ 2:45 AM

Marcus, Milan called me last night. She asked me if I had seen your Face Book page. I said "no, I'm not home." She said that there was a girl that made a comment on your page and that it suggested that you were a father. I told Milan that "I was currently driving at the time but I am on my way home and I will look at it when I get there." So, I start reading your page and there is this girl named Kierra that makes a statement, this is what she said: "Hey Babe, it's sad that you are gone, I think about and miss you every day. And by the way....she looks just like you." Marcus, I don't need to tell you that I hit the floor. I sent her a message asking her what she meant by that "she looks just like you" comment. She contacted me back and said that she though that I knew about the baby, because you did. She thought that you had told me. She told me the baby's name, and that she was born on December 15, 2011. She said that she didn't want anybody to know about either her having a baby or about you being the father, but yet she puts it in one of the most public forms in the world....Face Book! Wow! I asked her to call me right away. I sent her several messages back-to-back trying to get her to call me, asking her to call me right away. She finally calls me this morning. We are making arrangements for me to be able to go and see the baby tomorrow morning. So I'll let you know what happens.

Marc, I know that you're grown, or at least you think you are, but why didn't you tell me? I know that I kept on you and Nigel about not making a grandmother until I'm 50, but damn, this is a baby. Wow, I just heard your voice saying "mom, you say that now," that just made me laugh. I love you Marcus, as much as it hurts not having you here, I can still find laughter in somethings that I think you'd say.

---

| , places and things | 🔍 |
|---|---|

**Kierra**　　　　　　　　　　+ New Message　✹ Actions ▾

Conversation started October 8, 2011

**Kierra**　　　　　　　　　　1:09pm
Hello Ms sykes, my name is Kierra. I used to live in harbor house. I used to come to your house when you lived in waterview to see marcus. Then I moved to east point. We'll I'm writing you to say God bless your heart and give you strengh to go threw something like this. And if you need anything, Im here. Marcus was my best friend he loved my children.Stay strong and pray.

**Kierra**　　　　　　　　　　1:11pm
You and your family are in my prayers.

January 23, 2012

**Joreen Schatze Sykes**　　　　8:51pm
Kierra, Hi. I need to ask this. You made a comment on Marcus's page telling him how much you miss him. You also said she looks just like you. Be truthful with me...what do you mean by this???

**Kierra**   + New Message   ⚙ Actions ▼

**Kierra**   9:09pm
yes i did and i didnt want ppl to find out anything. but me and marcus have been messing for 5 years. i thought you remembered me. but marcus knew i thought he told you. But i guess not. i just had her on dec 15. Her name is faith and she is marcus daughter. sorry for keeping it from you for so long. i knew you ben going threw alot. I just wanted to find the right time. I didnt want anybody to know like the whole face book.

**Joreen Schatze Sykes**   9:15pm
Kierra, I do remember you. Please call me.

**Joreen Schatze Sykes**   9:42pm
KIERRA PLEASE CALL ME.

**Kierra**   9:44pm
ok

**Joreen Schatze Sykes**   9:45pm
CELL                    . HOME

**Joreen Schatze Sykes**   10:42pm
Kierra, please call me, Im waiting. if you need me to call you give me your number.

Kierra, I don't mean to be pushy, but you put something heavy on my heart, and I need more

## Wednesday, January 25, 2012

Marcus, Marcus, Marcus! All I can do is shake my head. This is some real life baby-momma-drama shit you got me caught up in! I went to go see Kierra and the baby today or at least attempted to. All I can do is shake my head at all this foolishness.  I went to pick Kierra up at Dover Down Hotel, why she was there is beyond me. She sat me down in the lobby, because she said that she wanted to talk to me before we went to go see the baby. So she tells me that she is having hard times, and that she is homeless at the time, and on and on.

Then she tells me that when she had the baby, she was going to give it up for adoption, but there were some circumstances around it that prevented her from doing so. Anyway, she goes on to tell me that she was living in some hotel with the baby, and the police came and took the baby. She said that she thinks that either the hospital or the hotel management might have called Child Protective Services on her because she was living in a hotel with a new born baby. Marcus the hairs on the back of my neck stood up. It just wasn't sounding right.

Anyway, she goes on to tell me that the baby is staying at a "friends" house in Capital Green. She tells me other things about her situation, but I can't remember everything that she said, it was just a long drawn out sad sob story, I just wanted to go see the baby. So afterwards, we drive out to her so-called friend's house to see the baby, and she's not there, so she leaves her a note in the door. So I took her to get something to eat for lunch and we rode around talking and getting to know each other. We ride back by the house again, still not home. So the third time we go to her house, she's home. I tell Kierra, to go up to the door and make sure that it's okay that I can see the baby, because it was late in the afternoon, around 5:30 and it was getting dark. I felt just a little uncomfortable going to some ladies house who doesn't know me, I thought that would have been just a little rude just to show up like that, and she doesn't know me from a can of paint, so I waited in the car for her to say it was ok for me to come in. About 10 minutes went by, and she was still standing at the door talking to her. It looked like they were in a heated argument, so I rolled the car window down to hear what they were saying, and I could hear them arguing. I got out the car to walk up there, I said "excuse me, I don't know what's going on and I don't mean to be rude or cause any problems, but my name is Joreen and the baby might be my granddaughter", or I think I said that I might be the baby's grandmother, something like that. Marcus, you should have seen her face, OMG! The shit done hit the fan now! I can't remember the whole entire conversation, but this is what I do remember. She looked me square in my face and said don't believe a damn thing Kierra is telling me. She said her name is Valerie, so Ms. Valerie was under the impression that she was the grandmother. Kierra told her that her son was the father of the baby. Marcus, this is where I think you made a bad decision in girls. This lady goes on to tell me about how she got placement of the baby, is because Kierra tried to sell the baby for money to some people in Chester. Ms. Valerie said that she went to Chester PA to get the baby from the people who were trying to buy her, Now if money actually transferred hands, I don't know.  But the lady told me that she told the people that if they didn't hand the baby over that she was going to call the police and tell them that the baby is being sold in black market, it was just a hot mess! She then tells me that she had to file for emergency guardianship or emergency placement of the baby with child protective services and that's how she came to have the baby. Now I don't know how much of that is true, and believe me, she told me a lot more than this, but this is what she is telling me. She did tell me how Kierra was staying with her after she had the baby (even though Kierra told me that she was staying in a hotel), and how her son and Kierra would argue. She also told me, that after her son and Kierra fell apart and Kierra moved out, then all of a sudden, the baby has a different father, so now there are three possible fathers. Any way it just went on. But by the end of it all, she didn't allow me to see the baby. But you know what also gets me Marcus, we must have stood there for about 20 to 30 minutes going back and forth, this lady telling me all this stuff about Kierra and how she is and not to trust her, and not once, not once Marcus, did Kierra deny any of it, she just stood there like a deer in head lights. All that time when she was talking to me in the hotel about her situation, she not once told me that someone else could be the father, not once did she tell me that her child was in Child Protective Services! Not Once! Marcus so much was said today, my head could explode! I am just flabbergasted that Kierra had nothing to say, even in the car when I took her back to the hotel, she didn't say anything about what this lady was saying about her. I should have known right then, I should have backed away. But I wasn't about to abandon the thought or the possibility that this could be my grandchild, the seed has been planted as some would say, let's see how it grows. But I am just so amazed that Kierra had nothing to say in her own defense, nothing to say, amazing. Whether what Ms. Valerie was saying was true or not, how do you just stand there and let people just talk about like that? Oh, I know how, you just do, because it's true.

So I talked to Pee-wee about her, because I knew that he knows Kierra, and he right off the back told me not to trust her. He told me not to believe anything that she says, and that he didn't know anything about her being pregnant with your baby. I also asked Jamere, and he said that he knew nothing about it either. But he did say that once you did bring up to him that you might be a father, but weeks later you came back and said no, it's not yours. I asked them first because I know that they are the closest to you, and if anyone would know, they would. But they knew nothing. Marcus I am in such disbelief right now, it's just blowing my mind. I mean what-the-fuck....REALLY!! I know you could have done better than this girl, I know you could have, I've seen you. But like what Mr. Garry would say, "it-is, what-it-is!"

So, I'm going to go through the steps to really see if this is your child, like I said, I can't just walk away from it now.

## Thursday, January 26, 2012 @ 10:30 PM

I miss you Marcus, I still have this strong feeling in my hands to want to touch your skin. My hands burn and sting, I'm constantly rubbing them. It feels like I need to touch you. I feel bad sometimes that I'm going on with my day, with my life as if you are not gone. I feel guilty about that. I only hope that you understand that all I am doing, trying to do, is for you.

As you know, I found out a day-or-two ago that you might have a daughter. Deep in my heart I so want it to be your daughter, my granddaughter!! That would be so wonderful. I just don't know. I think the mother is not being completely up front with me, I don't think that she knows who the father is. The mom is homeless and the baby is in foster care. I got the paperwork from court to establish guardianship. I have to admit though Marcus, the baby does somewhat look like you, the nose and the lips, but it's a baby, one month old, and you just don't know. It could just be me wanting to see you in her, but I'll tell you this much, I will fight for her! I hope that it's your daughter!

## Wednesday, February 1, 2012 @ 2:06 AM

Why do I keep waking up at this hour? I just can't sleep. Marcus I miss you so much. I wish you were here, I wish I could touch you. I have this sensation, a tingling in my hands that want to feel your skin. I am trying so hard to hold my feelings in and not have anyone see how I'm feeling on the inside. Day after day I just want to cry. And today I just couldn't hold it in anymore. Now I'm dealing with Kierra and your baby momma drama, wondering if the baby is yours or not. Marcus.... what were you thinking? I've always told you to use a condom. If the baby is yours I'm going to fight for custody. Given her current living situation and all of the other problems she's having, I don't think custody would be difficult. I'm trying not to get my emotions about the baby to involved, but it's hard. Honestly Marc if this is not your daughter, I don't know if I could take another hit.

I want to see you again Marcus, I just need to know that you are alright. I know that I'm working on your foundation, but I just don't know what to do with myself. There are so many different things I want and need to happen with the foundation but can't get the help I need. I know people have their own lives, but don't make a commitment to volunteer or do something if you know you can't or really don't want to do it, (lip service is all that is). The only person that picked up on my disappointment from Tuesday night's meeting at the library was Kenya and she called me tonight to talk about it and to see how I was feeling. Yes it was disappointing, and with everything else going on with the baby, Nigel, you and the foundation it hurts more. A small part of me wants to give up because no one is going to have the commitment or attachment to the cause like I do.

I know that the foundation is something that I wanted to do in your honor of you, and yes I know that it takes time to start a business "this is not my first time at the rodeo."

It's just that, when you share your passion for something with people and they verbally say that they want to join you in your venture, because YOU were like Family to them, then they are a no show, what am I to think? It's not like I can't do this without them, I'm just saying.

## Thursday, February 3, 2012 @ 11:15 PM

I had a bad day yesterday. I was feeling to bad to sit and write to you. My mind was all over the place. I didn't have one consistent thought, I was aggravated and irritated. I didn't want to talk or be bothered by anyone yesterday. The past few days have taken its toll on me. Everything just got over-whelming and I couldn't deal. I am however, feeling just a little better today, but still not completely functional. I woke up, had breakfast, went for a quick walk, I tried to get some work done, but couldn't. Went back to sleep, woke up feeling just a little better. I think that tomorrow will be better for me.

I keep having visual images and thoughts of October 8th, when I got that knock on the door at about 4:45 in the morning, Diane is telling me that you had just been killed. I keep having full images in my head of that very moment. I can't stop thinking about that. I keep having flashes/images in my head of what your body must have been going through. I wonder if you might of known who did this to you. I wish I was there holding your hand, just to tell you how much I love you. I hope that you didn't feel any pain. I hope that your mind was blank. I miss you so much. You know I can't help but wonder if that dream I had two years ago with dad sitting in his car crying out, "monster, monster" was a sign warning me about you. Maybe he was trying to say to me....Marcus, Marcus, and the fact that he was sitting in his car was also a clue, because you were near your car. It's just weird that they both tie into each other. I think that dream about dad, was truly all about you.

I wish you had called me that night and told me that you were stranded. You would call me for anything else if you needed it. Why didn't you call me this time? I am so mad at you for not calling me. I still sometimes can't stand to go into your room. I don't want to open the door; I'm scared that you're not there. I want you back so bad. I love you Marcus, I love you so much.

## Wednesday, February 15, 2012 @ 11:50 PM

Marcus I am having such a hard time today. I have been shaking all day, literally, from the inside, just shaking. I'm not going to talk much tonight. I just wanted to tell you that we had court today. It was for a Proof Positive Hearing. It's for the courts to determine why they should continue to be held without bail being set. Now I don't know if I told you this or not, but when we went to court to hear the case against them (this is just so fucked up), but when they questioned Kurt Dupree while he was being detained in Maryland, I don't know all what questions were asked, but I'm sure mostly if not all were about your case. After being questioned, Kurt Dupree goes and calls Lionel Williamson on the phone, the prison phone, he calls Lionel Williamson's girlfriend or someone who could walk across the street to where he was to give him the phone, he tells Lionel Williamson that the police know who he is, I can't remember everything that was said in court word for word but, basically he tells Lionel Williamson to tell the police that the gun in the picture was a toy or a fake.

There were some other things that Kurt Dupree told Lionel Williamson to say if/when he gets arrested. Now Marcus, you know that prison phone calls are recorded right? Don't get me wrong Marcus, I'm grateful and thankful for him doing this, but this was an act of pure stupidity. This was a scene straight from the TV show, Worlds Dumbest Criminals. But this idiot Lionel Williamson tells the police everything that Kurt Dupree told him to say. And all of it was evidence from the prison phone recording. They evidently had some picture from one of their cell phones that had four people in it and one of them was holding a gun that matched the description of the one that was seen the night that they took you. I think it was a silver .38, or something close to it, I'm not sure, I have to go back and look at the some of the reports that I have. Anyway, they had all this, that whole conversation on tape as evidence. Thank God for stupid people like that!

They told me right off the back that Warren Brooks was going to testify against Lionel Williamson. The way they said it, it was like he gave in, he was willing to testify. And even though Kurt Dupree is also going to testify, they said that Kurt Dupree couldn't be trusted to tell the truth, that he often times gives misleading information, and not just in your case.

## Friday, February 17, 2012 @ 3:05 AM

Hey Marcus, as you can see, I'm up again, I can't sleep. It's been happening like this almost every night for the past 2 months. I can't explain why. I go to sleep late so that I'm nice and tired, but that doesn't work.

As you know, your birthday is in a few weeks, Adrian

is helping to plan a party for you at the Sheraton Hotel. I told you that you should have married her. But she will always be my almost daughter in law.

There is a court hearing on Tuesday. It's for bail review for Lionel Williamson, Kurt Dupree and Warren Brooks. I really wish that this whole thing would be over with and they could just rot where they are.

I have been working hard on your foundation. I go to Garry for a lot of help and advice. But he criticizes me all the time and it make me not want to go to him for help. I know that he means well, but sometimes I don't think he realizes what he says to me, or how he says it to me, but deep down I know he means well. There are still a lot of things that I need to get done. But I am at a standstill sort-of. I'm finding that a lot of your friends are not really there like I thought or like they said they would be. But that's my fault for expecting so much from them.

Marcus I know I have not talked to you in a few days, weeks, but I am going to try to go back to sleep right now, I promise I won't stay away so long next time ok, I love you.


## Sunday, February 19, 2012 @ 4:15 AM

Marcus, I don't think that I am going to make it, emotionally. I feel like I am trying so hard to hold on and keep myself together. I feel like I could lose it all at any time. I know that I am using the foundation to hide behind and not face my feelings. It's not a good feeling. I was just lying here thinking about what would happen if I just let go. And you know Marcus, I feel ashamed to say this, but when I think about letting go I think about Nigel and it's not enough to keep me here. As much as I love Nigel too, I need both of you in my life. And then I think about or try not to think about what it's going to do to me if this baby girl is not your daughter. I will be absolutely crushed! I have been trying not to get my emotions to involved with this baby.

What I didn't tell you is that I keep having these crying spells for about 10 to 15 minutes at a time, day, night, middle of the afternoon, 5 o'clock in the morning, it doesn't matter when. There were a couple of times, I woke up crying...right out of my sleep. It feels like it's getting harder for me again. And I'm scared to share my feelings with anyone. People say they understand, but I know that they really don't! I don't want to pretend to feel that I can relate to them just because they say they understand. Even with people that I've met that have gone through the same thing. Everyone is different, what affects me might be different for them. And I hate to be rude. We might have similar feelings and emotions, but it's not the same. But I can understand what it is that they want or are trying to say. I mean we all bereave our children but the emotions are just different, that's why we are called individuals, because people experience things differently. Well it's about 4:40 in the morning now, again, I am going to try to go back to sleep. I love you Marcus.

**Monday, February 20, 2012 @ 6:30 PM**

Marcus, sometimes your friends will contact me, or they will see me, and everybody has a notion or the answer about what happen or why this happen to you. Everybody claims to have the inside scoop. Sometimes I wish they would all just leave me alone. Or better yet, go to the police about what they know, what good is it doing for me except make me feel worse than I already do? I've heard that about 3 or 4 people are claiming to have killed you. I'm hearing that someone put a hit out on you; I'm hearing that it was over that girl Emily. I'm hearing that people knew what was going down before it happened. And everybody seems to know why, you had a fight with this person, a disagreement with that person, I'm getting all this back and forth, he say, she say shit. Just go to the damn police.

## Tuesday, February 21, 2012 @ 9:15 PM

Want to hear something strange Marcus? The life insurance company paid on your insurance policy. I received the check in the mail today, when I opened It, it took me a minute to realize what it was. I mean, I knew it was a check for you, but it took a minute or two for it just to sink in. Once it did, I cried, because it represented loosing you all over again. It felt like it was blood money. It actually hurt receiving it. I didn't think that the insurance company was going to pay on your policy because it was so new. It was so new that they had not even delivered the policy to me yet. Remember that Saturday, when I hid your car keys from you, because the nurse was coming by to get blood work and stuff from you for the insurance policy that I was getting on you. Well, you passed away the day after they approved your policy, literally, the day after. When Marci filed the claim for me, we didn't even know at that point if your policy was even approved yet. Marci didn't even know yet, and she was our agent. So they said that they had to do some investigation, but that's typical of insurance policy claims within the first two years of opening. About a week after we filed the claimed in October, someone came to the house and questioned me as if I had something to do with you. They wanted to know, about my jobs, how much money I have, my investments, just all kinds of crazy questions. They weren't from the police department or anything like that; it's what insurance companies do when people file a claim, I guess to make sure that there is no fraud going on. Their timing and how they went about their investigation was just so insensitive and crude.

It's crazy to have received the check on a day when I had to deal with going to court for the bail hearings, it was just bad timing.

Why they would be considered for bail is beyond me! It's just the law I guess. It's more than likely that they won't get it, I hope, but still. The judge didn't make a decision; we will know in a couple of days, the AG's office will notify me. It was hard hearing all of the evidence again, hearing how and where you were shot. I broke down crying in the courtroom, just can't explain it! I wish there was a way you could tell us what happen to you.

## March 5, 2012 @ 4:00 PM

Kierra, just Face Booked me a message to tell me that the other boy is not the father. OMG Marcus. OMG!

## Monday, March 26, 2012 @ 8:20 PM

Hey Marcus, I miss you. Sorry that I have not come to see you in a while, I have had a lot going on building your foundation. I have had a long day today at the new office. I hope you're proud of me! I am really, really tired, I love you so much. I didn't write to you on your birthday, but your party was nice. Adrian helped me put it together, but she did most of it. Family and friends came out to celebrate but as always I expected more of your friends to come out then what did.  But, it is...what it is!  I tried to make a documentary video of your family and friends giving a testimonial or remembrance of you. But it was not recorded like I wanted it. I wanted people to sit individually, in front of the camera, but Garry had other ideas, and then everybody there didn't want to give a testimonial. So I am not going to use it on the Foundation's website.

Well, I still don't know anything yet about the baby. I think that a court date is coming up soon.  If she is your daughter, she is going to be so spoiled! Everyone else is doing ok, I guess, Nigel's court case is coming up in April, if there is anything that you can do from where you are...then work your magic! On the other hand, your foundation is almost up and running, we should be ready to roll out the office the first week in April, I can't wait!

## Monday, March 30, 2012 @ 7:47 AM

Hey Marcus, I dreamed about you last night, I dreamt that your death was a lie, and that you've only been away at work all this time with Peewee. In the dream you spoke to me and hugged me. This is how it went.....I can't remember where we was, but I am remembering a big field, a car (can't remember what kind of car it was), but after finding out about your death, I was so distraught, (like I am now) and you had come home. Everybody had been told and notified that you had died. So a few days had passed and you and Pee-wee came home, I couldn't believe that it was you.  You already knew what had happen and what was being said about you, but no one knew that you were still alive except for Pee-wee. I remember holding you so tight; I didn't want to let you go. Because you are taller than me, I made you sit on my lap, and I just remember holding and hugging you for a long time. You kept saying "Mom I'm ok, Mom I'm ok," and that "you love me." I can remember how you felt, having my arms around you. I just didn't want to let you go. You said that you had to leave, that you and Pee-wee had somewhere to go, and that made me very upset because you wouldn't say when you would be back, but I still just kept holding you. I can remember holding you then letting you go. A car was sitting out in the middle of the a field, it was a sunny day, spring or summer, then the car was gone, I was looking out into a field of flowers, and then you were gone. At that point the house phone rang and I woke up. You know that once you wake up from a dream, you can't go back to it. But I wonder if this is another dream that has a message for me.

## Tuesday, May 1, 2012 @ 2:15 PM

Hey Marcus, I had emergency surgery over the weekend. I had to have my gallbladder removed. I'm so glad that Garry just so happen to come over, or I would probably still be lying on the floor right now. I had Popeyes Chicken for dinner Saturday night, but the Doctors said that I could have eaten a salad that night and it still would have burst. I had server back pain. You know that I have always suffered from back pains my whole life, so when my back started hurting I really didn't pay it much mind. I just did my usual and took some 800mg of Ibuprofen, but it got worse, so I put my tens unit on, the pain got worst. No matter what I did my back pain was really hurting. Then

I started throwing-up, it smelled like the chicken I had ate. But then I just couldn't stop throwing up. Marcus at that point I was crawling on the floor in pain. If Garry wasn't here, I would have not called for help, because I just thought that it was my back. So we decided to go to the hospital around 10 or 11 I think. OMG Marcus, I think Garry took every turn with force, it felt like he was tossing me around in the car; that was the worst car ride ever.  After I had the surgery, the Dr. said that it was good that I came when I did, once they took out my gallbladder, he said that it was worse off than they thought. He said that I had a high fever because of the contamination it was causing in my body from it bursting and letting it go for as long as I did. Even though they said that it was not the chicken I ate that night, you know that I ain't eating fast food chicken again right?! OMG and the hospital, I will never go to Wilmington Hospital again! I don't care if I have to drive 20 miles to the next hospital, I will not ever go to Wilmington Hospital again! They were not only doing construction in the hospital, but they put me in a room with this lady that had company the entire time that I was there, the entire time! And they were LOUD! Marc I got out of surgery around 7 or 8 am, I still have Anesthesia in my system, I wanted to go to sleep. These people had no consideration at all! They just talked and talked and talked, non-stop. I kid you not when I tell you that there was someone there the entire time! I kept the drapes or curtains closed because my bed was closer to the door, do you know that twice, at to different times, twice, the guy that was visiting with her walked into my bed? I mean, he walked into my bed as if it wasn't there. You would think that he would walk around the curtain or in front of the curtain, all I heard was bam, right into my bed, what the hell, scared the shit out of me, and I just couldn't get any sleep, he ruined that. How does someone just walk right into your bed? I think he did it on purpose. I asked the two nurses if they could switch me to a different room, but they said that because of the construction, there were no rooms available. Oh, which reminds me, not only could I not get any sleep because of their constant talking and laughing, the construction was also keeping me up, the drilling and banging all day. I was so tired I just wanted to cry.

## Monday, May 15, 2012 @ 8:45 PM

Marcus, I am so sorry for you, your body was tortured. I found out today what took your life. I had an appointment with the AG's office today, and they were giving me a follow-up on your case. I asked a lot of questions as to what is going to happen next, and the process of things. I told them about the baby, they told me that the ME's office would have your blood. But about that later. Anyway, they told me that what took you was that overall, in addition to other complications, the main thing that took your life was that you had a bullet to your heart. When they told me that, Marcus my heart broke. You just don't know how much it hurts me to know that you had to go through this. I still find myself crying at any given moment about it. I can't escape this feeling. I drive and cry, I wake up in the mornings, and I'm crying. I still wake up almost every other night, 2, 3 or 4 o'clock in the morning with you on my mind. I sit in my office and think about you, trying to imagine what your last days were like for you. I think about the last time we spoke to each other on the phone. I said I love you Marc, and you said I love you too. You know that this happening to you only means that you're a better man than those three idiots?

Oh yeah, Jamere and Stephanie were here a couple of days ago. Jamere took that poster that was over top of your room door, the one with the big yellow smiley face that said "Thank You For Riding, Have A Nice Day" on it. Katelyn, their daughter was with them, she remembers you. She said that she misses you. Their baby shower is this weekend. As you know they are having a boy. Jamere wants to name him after you, but Steph wants to name him after her grandfather. You know what I'm wishing for right?

Now as for your possible daughter, the test results came back inconclusive, but it suggest that the baby is not yours. The testing center said that it doesn't mean that she's not your daughter. I used a 3rd party testing center, you know, like the ones they use on the TV shows. How they do their testing is by mouth swab. So this testing is tested through grandparent to child and not parent to child. So I'm just going to let the court system take over the case at this point. Since the ME's office has your blood, it can be parent to child testing instead of child to grandparent. This process will take a little longer, but if she is really your daughter, it will be worth it.

### Sunday, May 20, 2012 @ 5:10 AM

Marcus, I wish I knew what these dreams are all about. I had another one last night. This one was rather short. I dreamt that I was at Grandma's house and three people came to the house to see you, two guys and one girl. Anyway, they knocked on the door and asked for you, I said "I'm sorry but, Marcus passed away a few months ago." As they stood in the door way, the girl is standing in the middle, and the guys are standing on each side of her. Now, when I tell them that you had passed away, the girl, she had this surprised look on her face, her eyes got wide, her mouth dropped open, surprised and speechless. The guy to my right, on the girls left, quickly turned away and mumbled, Nooooo, in a surprised tone! But the guy to my left, he gave me this strange look. He had this smirk on his face, I would say that it was kind of like an evil look, but at the same time it was this look like.....he was up to something, and he was looking me up and down real slow. All of a sudden, I felt your presence behind me on my left. Now, even though I was standing in the doorway looking at these three people, all of a sudden, I was repositioned behind you so at this point, I'm actually looking at both of us from behind. (I'm looking at you standing behind me) Now, the me, that's standing in the door way, I turn my head to look back at you, you are standing to my left. I turned to look at you and your face is staring straight at the three people, not once did you look down at me, because you are taller than me, but you are just looking straight forward. Now even though I'm looking back at you, I still feel that I am standing behind you watching all of this. So, you are looking straight forward at these people and what you say and do next is what bothers me. You are standing behind me to my left and your right forearm is right about at the level of my stomach, and you push me back, and at the same time that you are pushing me, you say "mom, go in the house," and the sound of your voice was almost mean, angry. And it is at that point when I wake up, when I felt you touch me. The me that's standing behind you, is watching all of this, and the look that is on your face and the sound of your voice is a stern. You never looked directly at me, you just keep looking straight ahead at these people, they couldn't see you of course. But I woke up right at that point when I felt you touch me. I feel that you are trying to protect me from something or someone. Lately, I feel like every dream I have is a sign of something.

## Wednesday, May 30, 2012 @ 8:15 PM

Marcus, I know that you are going to be disappointed and angry at me for doing this, but  a few times, Kierra has called me asking me for some assistance, a few times she has asked me for money to help her get a hotel room, because she has no place to go. And I have been helping her out here and there. Marcus, I know, I know, I know! So she calls me the other day because she needed a room and it was race weekend at Dover Downs, she was trying to get the room early, because on Friday the rates go up, and the rooms are pre-booked. So I help her out again, but I told her before I left, I said to her, "that I don't mind helping you out, but until we find out if the baby belongs to Marcus or not, I can't do anything else for you anymore, I hope you understand." She said "oh okay, it's no problem, I really appreciate everything that you have done for me, I understand." Now she did not appear to be mad or anything, not that she had a reason to, but she seemed to be okay with what I told her. So about a week later when I went to go see and visit with the baby at Ms. Valerie's house, she tells me that Kierra has been going around telling people that the baby is not yours! What the hell! She said that the only reason why I want to have the baby is so that I can have a piece of you in my life, (I'm saying to myself, no shit!) She was saying that I live poor, that I have no money, just a whole bunch of bull shit. Can you believe this bitch? I have been giving her money because she has no place to live, but I'm the poor one, really! I tell her that I'm not going to give her any more money, now All-Of-A-Sudden, you are not the father. That bitch knew all along that you were not the father. Marcus she was talking so much trash about me. I'm the one driving around in a $40k automobile, I'm the one going out helping her to buy her personal female items, but I'm the one not living right. I'm not the one who's 22 years old with 5 kids, different baby daddy's, with no place to live, and giving my new-born baby up for adoption, getting arrested and calling me to help come get her out of jail, is this bitch for real? Again Marcus I ask you, what the fuck were you thinking?

The blood test for the other guy, came back negative, he's not the father. Ms. Valerie was so disappointed, she has been taking care of the baby almost since she was born, and now she finds out that the baby isn't her son's. I feel for her, but at the same time I'm elated, because that just might mean that the baby is yours. Honestly, I don't think she even knows who the baby father really is.

Yes, it's fucked up that she said, what she said, but I am still going to go through with the court hearings, again, I just don't know, and I don't want it hanging over my head...."what If". I want; I need for it to be a definite, yes or no, if this is your child.

### Monday, July, 9, 2012 @ 12:50 AM

Marcus, it's not okay, I don't care what you think or say, it's not okay, I want you home. I miss you!

### Friday, July 13, 2012 @ 10:15 PM

Marcus, I don't know what to do. I miss you and Nigel so much. Nigel has to do a lot of years. Nigel's whole life is gone, you're gone! I never would have thought I would be without the both of you. I was driving home from Dover the other day, and I got to thinking about all the times you must have driven the same route, back and forth from Dover to Wilmington, thinking about it just makes me want to drive into a tree. I'm still waking up between 2:30 and 3:30 in the A.M. Lately I can go right back to sleep with-in about 30 minutes. Last week, I couldn't go back to sleep at all, I was so tired. I took two days off from the foundation. I didn't tell Garry that this is why I took the time off though. I think he still doesn't understand how I'm feeling. I try to hide it most of the time, well, all the time from him and everyone. I guess this may be giving people the impression that I'm getting better or that I'm ok, when in reality, I feel like my insides are in a million pieces.

Lately, I have been sitting in your room, which is not easy, but I still feel your presence here, I can still smell you. Marcus it hurt so much, I just want the pain to stop, I want the pain to stop, but I can't leave Nigel here all alone.

## Saturday, July 14, 2012 @ 8:20 PM

Hey Marcus, what are you doing? I am just sitting here thinking about you, as always. I wish I could just put my arms around you and give you a giant hug. I miss you so much. Things are just not the same without you here. I miss you coming home, walking in the house all hours of the night, I don't know how everybody else feels, but I need that again. You never know how much a person is needed in your life until they are gone. I know that Jessica and Jamere really miss you too. Oh yeah, I'm about to get a tattoo of you on my back near my neck in the middle. It's going to be of your face. I think you'll like it.

I still don't know anything about the baby yet. I go to

court on the 13th of August for the guardianship papers I filed. I hope to finally know something about paternity by then. But I am still trying not to get my hopes up. I can't remember how it happened, but Ms. Valerie, the other women who has been taken care of the baby contacted me. She has been letting me visit with the baby, and she is so precious. I try not to go by her house too often; I don't want to get too attached to the baby. But I can't help it. She is truly a pretty baby, but Marcus; tell me what you were thinking about in messing with that girl. She is a hot mess. I think, I don't know, but personally, I think that she is hooking, that's just my opinion.

But anyway, your Foundation is doing well. I hope you like all things that we are trying to do with the kids. I thought that having a CPR class is a good ideal. With all the violence in the community lately, kids are quick to pull out a gun to shoot and kill someone, so I thought that with the CPR class for youth, it will teach them a greater respect for life, instead of them taking a life, let's teach them how to save one. You know Marcus, I am missing you so very much, that sometimes I have thoughts that after I really get this foundation really on its feet, I will give control of it to someone else and I will come be with you.

I just need to see you. I need to know that you are doing okay, and that you are safe. During the first couple of months, especially the first 3 or 4 weeks after you left, my breast were hurting so bad. After a mother gives birth to a baby, sometimes when they don't breast feed, their breast swell and hurt. At least it did for me. I remember it very well, I didn't breast feed you and the Dr. forgot to give me meds that would dry up my milk, and my breast would leak sometimes. I clearly remember the pain I had from it. They hurt to touch them; it hurt to lay on them when I was asleep. They hurt something like that now, every now and then, they will be real sensitive. I think my body is trying to separate you from me, I don't want it to. I want to still feel you and know that you are a part of me.

I heard something the other day...that a man is measured by the number of his enemies, but in fact the strength of a man is measured by those who loved him. If you are familiar with that quote, I know I just jacked it up. But I thought about you and all your friends.

## Tuesday, July 17, 2012 @ 6:05 PM

Hey Marcus, what are you doing today? I'm just a little angry today. You know, from the beginning I wanted answers. I just had this need to know all the details to your case. I had been asking to view the surveillance tape from the gas station for a couple of reasons. The main reason why I wanted to see it was because I just wanted to see you. This was your last day alive, and I feel like I need to connect with that. I need to see you moving about, and people don't see or understand that. Garry and the attorneys don't think that I should view it, they all suggest strongly against it. They say that it will only be more traumatizing for me to see you get killed. It's not that I want to see you get killed Marcus, I just want to see you! The other reason why I want to see the video is because I have been talking to people about Delaware's no loitering law. I'm told that at the gas station, that there were quite a few people out there, coming and going. But how many at the exact time is just not clear to me. I wanted to work with someone that could aid or assist me in making some sort of change to that law. Because I believe in my heart Marcus, that if as many people that was out there, wasn't there, that you would have been more aware of your surroundings, and you would be with me here today! I believe that in my heart Marcus! I think that those idiots would not have taken that chance if less people were in that parking lot.

I have been talking to several people, and I really feel like I'm being brushed off and not taken seriously about it. I feel that establishments should be enforcing the no loitering signs that are posted on their buildings. If they don't and something happens on their property, then they should be held partially accountable. When it happen, the newspaper said, that gas station is known as a hangout for kids, when clubs let out. Where they got that information from I don't know, but if that is the case, then why does the gas station allow it? You would think that having that many young people just hanging out in front of their business would detract legitimate business. This is also why I want to see the tape for myself, because I can't speak on something that I am not completely sure about. Actually, I talked to a State/District Rep about what I want to do, and you know what he told me Marcus…..he said that I should just leave it alone! What The Hell! He said that business owners are not going to report loitering for fear of retaliation. Marcus I looked at him like he was crazy. I told him, that is the problem now, people don't want to speak up or speak out. So basically by him saying that to me, was him supporting street law, with that "don't snitch" bullshit! Marcus, I was floored that he even said that to me. He said some other things about why that law won't work and why I won't be able to make a difference with it, but I don't remember all of it because I just went into a state of shock after he said that. I just can't believe it! Who's to say that the police didn't just happen to be riding by and see a group of people, not getting gas, all in one spot at the same time. Who's to say that the police just didn't stop to check things out, ain't that their job? People don't gotta know that the establishment called the police to have them removed. Wow! Well needless to say, he couldn't help me. So I talked to a couple of other people and I didn't get the same answer but they just said that there is really nothing else to the no loitering law that can be different, that it's pretty much ok the way that it is. Again Marcus, I believe in my heart that if as many people were not out there LOITERING, that you would be here now. You would have seen something or noticed that something was about to go down, I honestly think that you would have been more aware of your surroundings. I honestly believe that. So no, the current no loitering is not effective, because in my eyes, the gas station allowed it.

All I know is that when some people want a law changed or a new law to be made, it gets done. Why am I being pushed aside?

**Tuesday, July 24, 2012 @ 9:30 PM**

Hey Marcus, just feeling a little sad today. We fired our secretary for the foundation today. She basically didn't support the foundation or our cause. She thought that I was trying to replace her, that I was going to fire her, and I wasn't. I am in the process of looking for interns to fill certain positions....positions that I know that she can't do. Positions like marketing, video production, web development, you know things like that. Anyway, I instructed her to contact Del State and get some information for me. So she interprets that as me trying to replace her. So instead of her talking to me about what she only thinks is going on, she made comments to her boyfriend through text messages about me. She was saying things like, I'm a liar; I'm trying to replace her; I got her finding her own replacement, but the one thing she said that pissed me off the most is the statement she made that "I'm trying to make a job out of my son's death." Marcus, that hurt me to my heart, especially when I went out on a limb hiring her. I basically hired her on the reference of a long-time friend. This friend shared with me some things about her that most people would probably turn away from if they knew about it. But noooo, because I trust my friend and her judgment, I went on and hired her anyway. But because of the some of the things that my friend was telling me about her, how I came about the information was no big surprise. I actually still would have kept her on if it was not for that one statement she made about you. I mean I liked her, and for the most part she did a good job, at least for what I could see that she could handle. She had her challenges, but nothing that she couldn't learn. But nope, that one statement did it for me, she's gone! In the mist of her and her boyfriend passing these text messages to each other, they must have had an argument. So he decides to hunt me down at the office just so that he could tell me about these text messages and show them to me on his phone. I mean he really must have been looking for me, because I didn't work today, I just so happen to stop by the office and there he is. So I asked him to text me the messages after he showed them to me. I talked to one of our board members about it, and we decided to let her go. And because I was too emotional, she took care of it. Because I was ready to just wrap my hands around her neck.

### Friday, August 10, 2012 @ 6:45 PM

Hey Marcus, what are you doing? So much is happening. I know that I don't talk to you about everything, but I am sure that you know and can see for yourself what's going on. But anyway, I go to court on Monday about the baby, but it's for the guardianship. The court hearing for the blood testing is not until the 22nd. I'm hoping that on Monday they move that hearing up and make it one case. I wish there was some kind of sign you could give me to tell me if she is your daughter or not, I guess only time will tell for now.

Hey, I'm told they caught the fourth person in your case. They have not told me yet who it is. Officer Spicer said that they have to officially charge him in your case before they can release any information about him to me.

Remember a couple of months ago when Nikki told me about this guy who is either making the claim, or is said to be the one who actually put a hit out on you? Well, when Nikki told me, I kind of blew off the information, because it's just another name in a long list of names of he said, she said. Although it's Nikki, and I do want to think that she doesn't have a reliable source for information. Well, his name came up again. A few days ago, she told me about him again. I can't remember how the conversation came up, I think I was telling her how the youth golf program was going, how the kids where responding and acting and I was telling her who some of the kids parents were. And when I mentioned one particular parent's name, she said, "well, that's home bois" babies momma that I was telling you about before. The word on the street is that he put a hit out on Marcus". Nikki was telling me about him one day when I was at her job, and her source just so happen to come in that same day to give her some information about him (coincidental). Well, I instantly went and looked at the kids applications for the contact information, and sure enough, his name is there as the kids father. Marcus I was floored! My heart fell to my stomach. I could not believe it. I called Det. Spicer and asked him and he confirmed that "yes" this guy had been questioned as a suspect in your case. I told Det. Spicer that he has kids in the golf program. You know how this is making me feel right now, I'm angry, mad, upset, scared, all at the same time. Marcus I wish I could get revenge for you! I don't even know what this guy looks like. Det. Spicer said that they didn't have enough evidence on him to arrest him, or charge him with anything. But just the fact that he was questioned as a possibility is enough for me! So now, I got to find a way to get his kids out of the program. It's not anything against them; it's just that I feel like now he is getting over on me twice, because his kids are in the program. And I am sure that he knows that his kids are in the Marcus L Ware Foundation's golf program, and he knows your name. And what if one day, he comes to watch his kids at one of the events, it's like he would be making a mockery of your program, laughing in my face, like ha, ha, I got your son, now do for my kids! And I don't even know what he looks like. I'm not having it! The kids gotta go! I hate to say it that way, but that's what it has to be. I told two friends about it, and they both agreed that I should somehow remove them from the program, if only for my own piece of mind.

I can't stand that the police know more than what they allowed to share with me, I just can't stand not knowing. I just need to know "who, what, when, where and why." I feel like I'm in the dark about everything. You know how I am, I'm nosey! I think that you must have really put your foot in someone's ass for them to want revenge on you like this. I just want to know why?

## Saturday, August 11, 2012 @ 8:50 AM

Hey Marcus, I see that you were here last night. I got up this morning and noticed that the toilet seat in your bathroom was up, sorry I missed you.

## Monday, August 13, 2012 @ 10:40 PM

Marcus I went to court today. This hearing was for the guardianship of for the baby. All I can say is that I could have just slapped her silly! Long story short, the judge is going to speed up the blood testing process. She made this hearing for paternity testing which is what I was hoping she would do. She is going to submit the court order to the ME's office requesting for your blood to be tested against the baby's, and we will get the notification by mail, so you will know when I know. Oh yeah, they didn't charge that 4th person that was in the car that night, I don't know why. Maybe they had the wrong person or lack of evidence I suppose, but people are crafty. I'm sure he talked his way out of it.

## Saturday, August 18, 2012 @ 11:25 AM

I just got done watching this movie called Dead Man Walking starring Sean Penn & Susan Sarandon. It was about a man on death row for the killing of two people. By the end of the movie, I realized that with all that I am doing with the organization, I still have a lot of hate and anger inside me for Lionel Williamson, Warren Brooks and Kurt Dupree. And I don't want to let go of it.

## Wednesday, August 22, 2012 @ 6:20 PM

I was thinking today during my 45 minute drive to Dover about how I just want to sit down and write Nigel a letter telling him how sorry I was for doing this. That it's just too hard being without both of my boys. I want to write how sorry I am for being selfish and that I'm not putting Marcus ahead of him, it's just that sometimes the pain is so unbearable, and that I know he will not fully understand until he has kids of his own, but I have to leave him now.

Marcus I ache for you every day, but how could I leave Nigel behind, he already feels that I don't care about him. It's just that I have been so consumed with your trial and the foundation, that I have somewhat neglected him. I don't mean to, I want him to understand that. Besides, other than him, who would notice or care that I'm gone?

## Monday, August 27, 2012 @ 5:45 AM

Wide awake again this morning. Marcus, I dreamt that Milan had a baby by you that died and you and Peewee buried it in an unmarked grave behind grandmom's house in Capital Park. In the dream Milan, myself and someone else was behind the house for some reason. I showed them where my club house that pop-pop built for me used to be when I was a kid. Pop-pops shed was no longer there. The backyard was fixed up and landscaped. Remember how the edges of the yard use to drop off like a cliff? Then the lake, a stream was just beyond that. Well, the ground was almost leveled off, but you could still see just a little drop off because they had not finished leveling out the ground yet, but the area was nicely grassed over and cut low. Well, Milan and the other person started walking back there and they almost fell just a bit off that drop, I told them to be careful, there is a stream and marsh back there. So walking back up to the house, I seen a queen size bed behind the screen porch in the back yard (Don't ask me why). The bed was fully put together, it had sheets and pillows on it, and it was made up, no blanket, and oddly it was covered with baby diapers. The diapers were still closed up and folded in a way like they had just come out of the bag, in other words they were new, clean diapers. Anyway, I looked around for Milan, and she was standing in this one area of the yard, kicking leaves with her feet like she was looking for something. Her hands were in her pants pockets; her mannerism was like she was being discreet, kind of nonchalant like, casual. I picked up one of the diapers and it was soaked with water, but I could tell they had not been used, so I thought they were there for a while and just got rained on. The next thing I know, I was back in the house, with you, and I was telling you about the bed behind the house and how crazy Milan was looking standing there kicking leaves like she was looking for something. You must have thought that I figured it out because then you just started telling me everything. I remember seeing your arms reaching straight out with your face turned away as if you were trying to stop me from slapping you because I was standing in front of you angry! You told me that Milan gave birth in that bed, but the baby had died and you and Peewee buried it in the backyard. And Milan was looking for the spot where you buried it. Marcus, I woke up gasping for air. I called Milan and asked her, she said yes, she was pregnant by you, but she had a miscarriage. Wow! I really can't believe this. What is this Marcus, what is this a sign of? Are you telling me that Kierra's baby is not yours? Was Milan really pregnant by you? This whole thing has got me shook. I don't know what to do right now.

## Tuesday, August 28, 2012 @ 1:15 AM

Marcus I am WIDE awake right now, so I know that this is not a dream, I know it can't be because I'm writing this, LOL, but I keep smelling that cologne you wear. Are you here with me? Garry is not here, so it has to be you. If it doesn't rain today I will come see you, or at the least I will drive by. I miss you so much. I wish you were here.

I was just thinking that you have come to me in my dreams a few times now about different things. But you have yet to come to me and tell me why or who did this to you. Why? Tell me something, in the one dream with the 2 guys and the girl, I think you were trying to warn me, but protect me too; does that have something to do with what happen to you? Help me dream about that.

## Thursday, August 30, 2012 @ 9:50 PM

Tomorrow I have to go to the AG's office. They want to talk about Kurt Dupree's plea bargain. I was told that it was going to be Warren Brooks who was going to plead out and testify against Lionel Williamson that he was the indeed the shooter. Kurt Dupree was the one that they said they could never get the truth out of. I want them all to fry in hell. If I had a way, I would kill them myself. There is nothing that he could plead for that I would be okay with. I want satisfaction, but you're gone, how do I get satisfaction from that. Nothing anyone could do or say would give me satisfaction.

## Monday, September 3, 2012 @ 3:55 PM

Marcus, can you believe this B.S.? I went to the AG's office on Friday to discuss your case with them. They tell me that because of the lack of evidence and motive, that Warren Brooks and Kurt Dupree are basically going to get off easy. First of all Warren Brooks is only going to get 2 years for conspiracy, they said that in DE, 2 years is the maximum time you can get for conspiracy. And by the time we get set to go to trial and he gets sentenced he will have time served and he'll get out. That is not justice! What about being charged as an accessory to a crime, or is that one-in-the same? He gets to walk around and act like nothing has happened. You will never again walk this earth, how is that justice? Marcus that is so not fair! Kurt Dupree is getting charged with conspiracy also, but in addition to that he will get 10 years, but those 10 years are for some other charges that he had pending that had nothing to do with you. You just don't know how angry this makes me. I was so upset when we were all sitting at the table, that my nerves had my stomach all tied up in knots. You know how I get when I get real stressed, or maybe you don't, getting over emotional, or stressed, upsets my stomach like crazy. My stomach just turns and turns, I had to shit so bad! My stress, my nerves was all in my stomach. I didn't say too much, I just put my head down on the table and cried, Garry said a lot and asked questions. I'm glad that he was there. I just couldn't believe what I was hearing. This was the plea bargain that they agreed to, and also in turn they both are going to testify against Lionel Williamson. They both are going to testify that he was the shooter. So he is going to get death or life, supposedly! They said that they don't have enough information or prove that they had prior knowledge of what was going on. My question is, if Kurt Dupree was the driver, he had enough knowledge that right after the shooting, he drove the car away, with the head lights off, behind the gas station to find and pick up Lionel Williamson, somewhere by Home Depot, how is that not having enough knowledge, how would he know to do that? I don't know the law, but I think that if you ask anyone, or give anyone that scenario, they will say the same thing, he knew! And for that, he only gets 2 years timed served I think that any other person, in the same situation heard gun shots, the first thing they would do is duck and hide. If I were sitting in my car and I heard gun shots the first thing I would do is, duck and hide! And yes, I might even drive away to avoid getting shot myself, but only after I got up from hiding on the floor of my car, and definitely not to drive with my lights off to see where the shooter went. I'm sorry; I'm not the kind of person that runs towards commotion while right in the middle of it. But no wait, how about this Marc, Warren Brooks is standing out in front of the gas stations entrance doors talking to some damn girl on the phone, and this girl just so happen to be parked right next to your car. So he's on the phone talking to this girl and just before, right before it happens, he tells the girl that she'd better move because something is about to happen. So she moves her car. What the fuck is that Marcus? Really! And they want to spin this bullshit that they didn't have prior knowledge. This whole thing is just so fucked up. Marcus I'm sorry that I am cursing so much, I'm just so mad right now!

But anyway, I am so heartbroken that this is all they are going to get. From the beginning, they kept telling me that they are going to be charged with this-that and the-other, and now they are just getting a slap on the hand. I know that I can't blame the attorneys for any of it, the facts are the facts, it's just how the law is written. Laws need to change! I think that in cases like yours, that the Family (meaning me) should have some influence on what should happen. I even told them that I'm not for the death penalty, but I'm not against it either. I told them that I think that the punishment should fit the crime, but I also believe in and eye for an eye. As much as I want the three of them to die for what they did to you, I couldn't have someone else's death on my heart. I think that they should get life in prison without the chance for parole. I know that people have their own interpretation of the law and they can use it, twist it, and manipulate it to mean or accomplish what they want. Why not in this case? I just find it so hard to believe that here you have 3 maybe 4 people in a car; riding around together all night, and they claim to have no clue what Lionel Williamson was going to do that night. And to add fuel to the fire, Lionel Williamson and Warren Brooks, so I'm told, have committed crimes together before. What the hell! So I'm supposed to believe and just accept that they knew nothing about this? I don't think so! Never will I believe that!

Peewee stopped by Saturday afternoon, he misses you and Nigel. He said that he is trying to get his life together. And I still have not heard anything yet about the baby, but of course when I do, you will be the first to know. Every time I ask Peewee about Kierra, he just laughs and says don't trust her, she got tricks.

I was making a new DVD of your pictures and the video that Peewee made with his cell phone of you at the car wash, I think that I did a really, really good job putting it together. It started with your baby pictures and showed age progression, ending with your headstone. When I finally finished it, I kept watching it over and over. It made me sad and lonely for a while. I kept having feelings and thoughts that I wish I could touch you again. I started getting that burning and stinging feeling in my hands again like I did when you first left me. I just wanted to touch you so bad. I just want to talk to you again. Marcus please come home! I want you home with me and Nigel. I need you home.

## Monday, September 10, 2012 @ 8:40 PM

Marcus why am I being punished like this? What did I do so wrong in my life to deserve this? I had my first mammogram last week; I got the test results in today that showed that I have a mass in my left breast. I guess this is what I get for not breast feeding you and Nigel. Marcus I could just scream. I can just fall apart. Garry is here, and it is so hard right now pretending like I'm ok, I just want to scream, hit, punch! Why me Marcus, why now? My Dr. said that they will retest in 6 months because it was my first exam and they have nothing to compare it against.

## Thursday, September, 13, 2012 @ 6:25 PM

Marcus, I got your autopsy report from Dr. O's office today. I thought that I was not going to have access to it until after the trial. At least that is what the ME's office told me. Marcus, I am so sorry, I am so sorry that you had to go through that. Your body went through so much. I hope that you didn't suffer or feel any pain. My heart hit the floor when I read the report. I hate that you had to go through this. The report was very descriptive as to where the bullets entered your body, the direction they went in, and the organs they damaged. I had Dr. O. explain some of the terms to me. He said that to him as it reads, it was the bullet that ended up in your heart that took your life, although other organs were damaged, it was ultimately the one in your heart.

I am still so very disgusted and I feel so very violated that all of this examination of you happened before I was even able to see you. Pictures of your body were taken; you were poked at. Just thinking about it makes me angry. What ever happened to people being able to identify the body first? What if I wanted to donate any viable organs of yours to someone? I know that everything that night happened kind-of fast, but still. I heard of someone who had their child's heart cremated and she wore it in a locket type necklace. What if I wanted to do something like that? I just feel that from the beginning I have had no say so into anything in regards to you, and you are my son. I have so much anger and contempt for the way that this happened. They did all this and it took 2 days before I could see you. I feel so violated that I'm shaking inside just thinking about it.

Marcus I just wish I was there. I wish that you didn't have to die alone. I wish that I could have taken the pain and hurt away from you. I miss you so much. I want to be there with you wherever you are. I want to hug you and tell you it's ok. My life, my heart, doesn't feel the same without you. I still can't imagine my life without you. I miss your goofy laugh, you're always joking, coming in at all hours of the night, your music that I can't stand to hear. I miss how I would say "you know I don't like you right?' and you would say, "you don't gotta like me, you love me." Marcus it feels like bricks are sitting on my chest. Why you, why did it have to be you. Why not somebody else's child, why mine. I feel so alone without you and Nigel. I try to pretend that you're at work and Nigel is just out with some girl. I still hear you walking around the house at night. Marcus I can't tell you enough how sorry I am, I feel so guilty. I should have been there to protect you. I wished you had called AAA to help get your car started. I wish you had been home, I wish you would have called me. I wish you would come back! Sometimes I feel like I'm gonna lose it. It's like something inside of me is going to break. It's so hard holding that feeling inside. I don't know what I'll do if I can't keep holding on. If I think too much about you, I feel like I'm gonna throw up, but I don't want to stop thinking about you. I feel like if I stop thinking about you that I'll forget about you. The scent of you is almost gone from your room.

First, the boys Kurt Dupree and Warren Brooks only gets 2 years, and now I just read your death report. I don't know how much more I can take. Marcus you are so handsome. You could have had a good life. What will it take to make this pain go away? I go to sleep with you on my mind; I wake up with you on my mind. I walk through the house with you on my mind. I drive my car with you on my mind, sometimes I want to just drive into a tree, I take a deep breath and it hurts. Marcus my pain is so bad that I really don't want to feel it anymore. But I gotta keep thinking about Nigel. I can't leave Nigel, I'll be honest with you Marc, he is the only reason why I'm still here. I don't want him to be without either of us! How do I keep these feelings from building up? I don't want to be over them because that would mean I'm over what happen to you. And nothing is going to bring you back. I can't talk to any one because no one knows how I truly feel, even people who I've met that have had a child murdered. Yes, we all have pain but our pains are not the same. I'm not that strong Marcus, I don't know how else to explain that to people. We don't share the same emotions or feelings, yes they can relate to the hurt, to the pain of what I'm feeling. I JUST WISH PEOPLE KNEW WHAT I'M FEELING! No one knows that I want to kill myself right now. No one knows that all I want to do is not wake up. I feel like driving into a tree. I walk around all day smiling, laughing, like life goes on, but it's all a front. I don't even feel that way on the inside. I feel like little sharp spikes or pins are sticking me on the inside, right in the middle of my chest. I feel so alone, but I'd rather be alone then to have someone in my face telling me that they understand. And I know that they mean well, I just can't stand to hear it, they are only trying to be comforting, but they're not, it's not comforting! I do talk to people, they want to hug me to console me...don't touch me! That just makes it worse for me.

And then there are those people when you tell them what happened, you get this long  silent stare, like they are afraid to break eye contact with you, they have this bewildered look on their faces, like they are trying to find the right words to say. They don't know what to say or how to act or respond, but they just keep looking at you. And then they try to impart words of wisdom and encouragement on you, telling me that I'll get through this, that I'm a strong person, oh and my favorite, "Marcus would want you to move on." How would they know what you would want? They don't know you! Get out of my face and leave me alone! They want to tell me that you are with GOD now. Marcus, whatever belief I might-have had in GOD, trust me it's gone now. I know that people would be surprised to hear this, or say that I just lost my Faith, that I just have to believe in him. They don't know my pain. They don't know what I am experiencing.

What is eating at me Marcus, sometimes I'm scared of what is, and sometimes I want it to make itself more clear to me. Pictures, images of you keep going through my head of what your body must have been going through. Images of that night keep going through my head. It's almost like I was there. It's like I can actually see your body falling to the ground, I have images of the expression that you might have had on your face. I know that television and how they glorify these types of things have a lot to do with that. But this is the type of imagery I have in my head. From the start, I always wanted to know, I keep asking, I need to know, it's important for me to know who was with you. And I don't mean people that you just say hello or what's-up to, I mean someone of significant. So as far as I'm concerned, you died alone. I just need and want to know what, if any, were your last words? Did you say anything? Did you ask for me? I was told that there was a person there that you knew that was trying to perform CPR on you; I want to know who he was. I'm told that one of them was in the military. I want to talk to him. I want to know who the EMT people were. I just need to know that you were not in any pain. I want to know if you called out for me. There is just so much about that night I want to know.

I keep saying to myself that I wish I was there to hold your hand. I feel like I wasn't there for you, I abandoned you, I let you down, I messed up as being your mother, I didn't protect you. Why didn't I protect you when you needed me most? I am so sorry! I am so sorry that I wasn't there for you. You would call me for everything else under the sun, money, food, gas, come pick you up, Mom I'm going to Dover, can you take me to the bus station, why didn't you call me that night? I am so angry at you for not calling me. I will never forgive you for not calling me Marcus! Marcus I'm not supposed to be without my boys. I have nothing now. You're gone forever and Nigel is in jail. I can't have any more kids. I don't know yet if the baby is yours. I feel so lost and confused. I just want to be by myself, so that I don't have to pretend. If I want to cry, I can cry, if I want to scream from the top of my lungs, I'll scream, if I just want to lay in bed, I want to be able to do all this without anyone saying oh, you need to get up and out and do something. You need to do this, that or the other. I just want to be left alone, I just want to die. I want to die so much, I can't get through this. I thought that starting your foundation would be a good thing, that it would help me heal. It's NOT! I'm doing it to honor your name, and I think that you would want me to help other families and kids, so for that reason, I'm doing it.

Garry is here with me right now, and I feel like I'd rather be alone. Everything today is irritating me, my head hurts, I can't breathe through my nose. I just want to be alone. Nothing against him, and I know he just wants to help, comfort and spend time with me, making sure I'm ok, but I just want to be alone.

And on top of that, he's eating sunflower seeds; as much as you know how I love my sunflower seeds, just the sound of them cracking makes me want to scream right now. Crack, crack, crack, that's all I'm hearing right now! The sound of those damn seeds makes me want to cry. I took the clock off the wall because the sound of it ticking was making me irritable. I put it under some pillows. It's like every sound, every little minor sound is extra right now, enough already! I know that's petty, but it's how I feel, and I know that I should be confiding in Garry, especially about how I have been feeling, but again he is someone who truly doesn't understand how I am feeling. I love him, but I just want to be away from anyone who doesn't understand me, basically, that's about everyone. What is going to happen when I settle into these feelings, I am trying so hard to be strong.

## Saturday, September 15, 2012 @ 4:25 AM

Hey Marcus, I couldn't sleep again. I know that I can't replace you. But I'm feeling like I want another baby. Maybe it's just me feeling lonely.

## Tuesday, September 18, 2012 @ 9:50 PM

Hey Marc, I'm doing better today. I thought a lot about you today. One of your cousins did a bad thing. She and her mom must be going through a little tiff; she posted on Face Book how much she hates her mom. A lot of people responded to her post about what she did, she didn't say what happened between her and her mom, but it was just the fact that she posted "I hate my mom" on Face Book wasn't good. I sent her a message telling her how ashamed of her I am for doing that. And no matter what happens between her and her mother, is not reason to put your business in the street. You remember how big on privacy I am. Anyway, I tried to talk to her about how her mom is only trying to raise her to be a proper and respectful person. She should always cherish what you have because you never know when it might be gone. I told her how every day I think about and ask myself why didn't I protect you, where did I go wrong? I told her that I think I failed you. Even though I still have no answers to why this happen to you; and you were not doing anything wrong, people have the tendency to wonder if anything that they did in raising their child had anything to do with the type of lifestyle their child was living. I have wondered, if I had been a better person, a better mother, maybe I could have raised my children differently, given them a different lifestyle, and raised them in a different community. Or at least, this is how I felt. Since your death, my life has become full of what-ifs. And now that she made that statement on Face Book, she can't take it back. I told her it shows bad character on her part also, and I know that her mother raised her better than that! Anyway, my conversation with her made me think about all the little petty arguments you and I had. Some I'm sorry for, some I'm not, you can be a little hard-headed sometimes, LOL. I hope she apologizes to her mom, at least for posting their business in a public form, Face Book of all places.

## Saturday, September 22, 2012 @ 9:55 PM

I spent the day with you today. I changed around how your head stone looks. I dug up the dirt and removed all the weeds and grass. I lined your head stone with gray rocks, (gray landscaping rocks). It really looks nice. I know

you probably don't like it. I can just hear you saying, "Mom....what is this?" With that goofy smile on your face. But I like it, be mad all you want to. I know the other people that was out there was probably wondering what I was doing. I wonder if the property people are going to say something to me about it, but I don't care, I paid for that little piece of land, I own it, we'll see what happens, I'm not moving it that's for sure! I went to see Nigel yesterday; he still doesn't talk about you. I'm sure it's still hard for him, it's still hard for me. You know Marcus, sometimes I feel like there is nothing here for me anymore. But I won't get into that right now; I don't want to get emotional. I love you Marc.

## Friday, September 28, 2012 @ 6:10 PM

Marcus, I am so crushed. I hurt to my core! Warren Brooks is out of jail. I feel so lied to, I feel deceived. I wasn't even told that he had court. The prosecutors knew what was going on, I had to find out through a phone recording and e-mail from the VINE system, that he was released. They knew that he was going to get out; they couldn't call me to give the heads-up. They assured me that I would be informed of ALL court proceeding pertaining to you. They told me that the court hearing that he had that released him had nothing to do with your case; it had to do with other charges he was facing. How is that, if it had nothing to do with your case, why is it that he out? I think that they intentionally did not tell me. If it was all about another case and other charges he had, then why was your case reviewed. He should still be in jail just from your case alone, then I would have been there.

You are missing so much of your life and he gets to walk

around. I feel like they are trying to convince me that who they really want, who they really want to go after is the shooter, Lionel Williamson. They said that they don't have enough proof that Warren Brooks knew what was going on, that Lionel Williamson was about to shoot someone. They said that just because he was in the car, and made a phone call to a girl and actually warned her that something was about to happen, that wasn't enough for them to prove that he had prior knowledge about what was about to happen. Even though Kurt Dupree admitted that they went to a party looking for you, how is that not having prior knowledge?  And now here we are, he gets out, and Kurt Dupree only gets 10 years. And technically, those 10 years is not for you, those 10 years stems from prior charges he had, Kurt Dupree and Warren Brooks both got only 2 years for conspiracy. Conspiracy in Delaware only holds a 2 year sentence, so I'm told, so basically they are getting time served, and that's why Warren Brooks is out. To me conspiracy means when someone conspire together to do something. I think that's no different than being an accomplice.

Marcus, you so don't deserve to be treated like this. Oh Marc, why didn't you call me that night if you needed help with your car? I am so angry, so mad at you for not calling me! Why? You know I thought that this was going to be an easy case. I know that they don't have a lot of evidence from what they tell me, but with what they do have, should have locked this case up! They are telling me that Lionel Williamson is going to get either the death penalty or life in prison. But there is something inside me that says that he is not going to get either. I can feel it. I have a strong feeling that he is only going to get a slap on the wrist with 25 no more than 30 years or something like that. Marcus, if that happens, I don't know what I 'm going to do! That is just another slap in the face for me. Is this what your life is worth to them? You weren't a criminal, you were not out there doing illegal things, I don't think. You had a job, your own car; you were doing well for someone your age. Marcus, what do you want me to do? OMG, Marc, how am I going to tell Nigel, he is not going to take this well. He is already on the line with his feelings. Do you know how angry he is going to be if I tell him this? He is not going to take this well at all! I am already feeling sick to my stomach.

Marcus, memories of you are not enough. I need you here; I want to be with you. I ache for you so bad, you are my son, no one had the right to take you from me, no one! Sometimes I wish someone would do their family ill will! So they could feel like I do. Marcus I miss the sound of your voice, the funny way about you. There is just so much I miss about you that I wish I could have back. Why did it have to be you? I feel so alone without you and Nigel. Sometimes it's so hard just to get through the day. I'm so tired of pretending that things are ok with me, I hurt so bad inside. The pain I have is so hard to explain. My eyes are constantly holding back tears. I feel like if you say the wrong thing or anything at all, that I will just burst out crying. I want to go out into an open field, where it's just me, like on TV and scream so loud from the top and bottom of my lungs and no one can hear me. I feel like I need to release and can't.

## Monday, October 1, 2012 @ 9:55 PM

Well Marcus, here we are, we are coming up on one year since you've been gone 7 days away. You don't know how much I miss you; I'm at a loss for words right now.

Tomorrow is your Foundations 1st Annual Banquet Fundraiser. I hope it all goes well. We are honoring Dave Spicer and Diane Glenn from Dover PD. Dave headed up the investigation on your case, and Diane is who delivered your death notification to me. I love them both for all that they have done; they have helped me out a lot. I just hope that they are pleased with the event tomorrow. I want to do so much with helping other people in my situation, and they are a big part of me wanting to do that. I really hope they enjoy it.

### Wednesday, October 3, 2012 @ 6:15 AM

OMG Marcus, we had such a good time yesterday. I am just so pleased at how everything turned out. The food was great, the band was phenomenal! The stories that Doug Watts told about Dave touched me, even Kim, talking about Diane. I mean the whole night was just great. Food, entertainment, the program, it was just all great, well that's my opinion. I really enjoyed myself, the Mayor and the Chief of Police were there. A few other people that I have formed a business and personal relationship with were there, oh, family was there. Dave's wife Joyce and Diane's father and other family members were there too. The only thing that was missing was dancing, maybe next year. I gave Dave and Diane awards. But you know, for me this event was more personal than it was business. I really, really hope that they know how much I appreciate them. They mean more to me than just the two people that handled my case because it's their job. It's a lot more than that for me.

## Sunday, October 7, 2012 at 1:34 PM

Tomorrow will be one year since you've been gone. I thought that I would make it through with no problem, but this morning I woke up and my chest was hurting, my heart was beating so fast, I couldn't breathe. I felt as if I was being choked, well not choked but like something had a hold of my heart and was squeezing it tight. I miss you so much Marc. I have thought and contemplated so hard about taking my life. It would be so easy for me to do. You just don't know how many times I drive to Dover from Wilmington just wanting to drive off the road into a tree, crying as I think about doing it; my hands are shaking now just thinking about it. But I have Nigel, he needs me. I don't want to do that to him. He needs me, I need him.

If you didn't know, Warren Brooks is out of jail. You know how devastated I am about that. They said that in exchange for his plea for conspiracy that he is going to testify against Lionel Williamson at the trial. That doesn't comfort me in any way what so ever. He is on probation, but they will not share the details of his probation with me. But I know that he is not on house arrest. This whole thing is so unfair. What guarantee is there that he is even going to show up to the trial? If he doesn't show up, they are probably going to still continue with the trial, and just issue a bench warrant for his arrest. And by the time they catch him on that, the trial will be over, so they might only charge him with failure to appear or something like that, and just extend his probation, maybe.

I'm going to say this Marc; I should have trusted that if something like this was true, that you would have told me if you really thought that it was a real possibility that you was the father. The test results for the baby came in. She is NOT your daughter. Even though I continued with the whole process of going through with the blood testing after all the witch said about you and me, and you not being the father, I just had to follow through with it. But I'm not all that disappointed any more, I'm lying, yes I am! I wish that little girl was you daughter. But I wish that little one the best. She is going to be adopted by another family. And it does hurt, it hurts that she's not your daughter, and it hurts that someone could do that to someone else. That she would attack someone in this manner at the most vulnerable time in their life. To try to use someone's death as a personal gain.  I'm hurt and disgusted at the same time. Your seed is forever gone. I'm so angry! I can't hold back my tears. I have no part of you now. You can't give me grandchildren. I will never see your smile in another.

Your trial was supposed to be next month; it got pushed back to March. Jury selection begins on the 11th, and the trial begins the 18th, expecting to last 3 weeks. My optimism isn't all that high. I feel like I need to prepare myself now for disappointment.

**Wednesday, October 10, 2012 @ 9:30 AM**

I made it! I thought I was going to have a hard time getting through the past couple of days, but I'm here. I must have watched your DVD that I made of you at least 30 times yesterday. It wasn't easy. I pretty much didn't answer the phone all day. I really just wanted to be left alone. A lot of your friends left messages on your Face Book page. Jessica spent the day with Nikki. I was here all alone.

I wanted to drive to Dover on Monday and spend some

time with you, but I really couldn't deal. And the pills I've been taking kept me asleep for about 2 days. Anthony was in town, he stopped by to see you. He and a couple of his friends took pictures with you at the cemetery. I am going to visit with you tomorrow. I have a visit with Nigel on Friday.

## Thursday, October 11, 2012 @ 3:10 AM

You see what time it is? I thought I was past this. Why do I still keep waking up at this hour?

## Monday, October 15, 2012 @ 9:25 AM

Hi Marcus, I just wanted to tell you that I love you. Marcus I am so proud of you! You were hitting some tuff bumps in the road, but you were growing into such a man. I am still mad at you for not calling me that night to tell me that your car was broke down, but even so, I am still proud of the man you were becoming. This may sound corny, but if you were not already my son, and I didn't know you, if I was to meet you just out and about, I honestly, honestly would say that you are exactly the kind of son that I would want. But you are my son, and I love you, and I'm so proud of you.

## Friday, October, 26, 2012 @ 8:05 AM

I dreamt about you again last night. I don't remember how the dream started, but I dug you up because you had been calling for me to come get you. The next thing I remember is we were in something like an auditorium or movie theater style setting and you were lying down next to me in the seats. You weren't lying like as if you were dead, but more like you were asleep, on your side, knees bent, like in the fetal position with one arm under your head, like how I remember you slept. So, I go from digging you up, to seeing you lying next to me in the theater. I remember people sitting in the seats behind us, but don't recall if people were sitting in the seats in front of us. I had been in and out of the theatre for a couple of days, I kept leaving and coming back, but you never left that spot that you were laying in. What gets me is that you were alive, but you had not spoken to me, and you just laid there sleeping. Then I remember, I knelt down in front of you to wake you up and talk to you, I looked at your face and your hands, your skin just didn't look right, your tattoos looked funny, it looked as if everything was sinking in. And then I noticed how your body smelled and realized that something wasn't right with you. I left you laying there still sleeping for what seemed like a week in a movie theater and I went to talk to a counselor that I had been seeing. He had an office full of clients but I just barged in and fell to my knees in front of him where he was sitting. I laid my head in his lap and started to tell him what I did. He asked everyone in the room to leave except his secretary. We were talking, but his secretary decided to leave the room. He continued to say something to me. Some time had passed and the next thing I recall, we were watching you out of the window playing basketball by yourself, we must have been on the 2nd or 3rd floor, because we were looking down at you. You played different, slow, almost like we were watching you in slow motion, but you seemed normal. The next thing I remember was we were outside with you watching you play. And then this truck drives up, it looked something like a tow truck. My counselor was telling me that you had to go back but I didn't want you to. You walked over to us, my counselor said to you that you had to go back, and for the first time, for over a week or so since I had dug you up, you spoke. Your voice was the same, you just sounded like yourself. I don't recall seeing your braids, but when you spoke I could see inside of your mouth. Now even though your face looked normal, you looked as if nothing was wrong with you on the outside. The outer of your body was not deteriorated, you just look normal, you looked like Marcus. But when you spoke, looking inside of your mouth, it was all black and slimy, and half of your jaw had dropped down and was disfigured looking. But just looking at you, you were fine from the outside. It was just then when I had realized what I did by digging you up. The counselor told you that you needed to go back and you said that you didn't want to go back, that you wanted to stay with me. You said that you were old enough and that you had rights over your own body. Just then, the driver of the truck handed me something, a piece of paper or something, I don't really recall what it was exactly. My counselor said to you "yes that is true, but your mother has more rights, more say so then you do. " I looked at whatever it was that the driver gave me and it started to change, at first it was blank, clear, and then this image started to appear, it was the wording on your head stone. Right then I woke up crying.

What does this mean Marcus? Why did you come to me in this way? Why would you hurt me in this way? But it was good seeing you. Why Marcus, you know how much I want you back. This is why I don't want to be here without you. But I am trying so hard to be here for Nigel. It hurts my chest and head so bad, I'm trying to keep it together. It would be so much easier just not being here. Sometimes I want to bang my head against something hard just to block the pain and get through this. I want to bang my head to except what has happen to you. These up and down emotions I have hurt, and more than just an emotion pain, this is real physical pain. People just don't understand, they don't have a clue as to the hurt, anger, pain, worthlessness, that I have inside me. I laugh and I smile in front of people, but I'm falling apart inside. I'm just not me! I wish I could feel on the inside, how I appear to be on the outside...happy.

## Thursday, November 1, 2012 @ 8:05 PM

Hey Marcus, just a quick note, I just wanted to tell you something that has been going on in my mind for a couple of days now. The other day I said to Garry that I was lonely, well this is the exact way how I said it: "Now that Marcus is gone and Nigel is away, I'm lonely. Just knowing that Marcus can't give me grandkids and it will be a while before Nigel will be able to. And even though when it was a possibility that the baby might have been Marcus's, I was really looking forward to being a grandmother. Just thinking about it makes me lonely." Now, if that is not exact as to how I'm feeling, I don't know how else to explain it to him, but noooo, what does he do, turn it around to make it about him. He said, "Yeah, I guess you are lonely when I'm not here." How I am feeling has nothing to do with him! My loneliness is nothing he can fulfill. There is a part of me that's just gone, just not there anymore. I have a hole in my heart, an emptiness that he just can't touch. I don't mean to excuse the feelings we have for each other, and it's not to say that I don't miss him when he's not here, because I do. It's just a different kind of feeling; this is the loneliness for my child, not my significant other. They are just two different feelings, two different emotions. My feelings had nothing to do with him, so I just got a little uptight that he would take my emotions about you and Ni and make it about him. I'm expressing my feelings about not having any grandkids, about not having my boys. I don't know, maybe I'm just being over emotional about it. I know what he was trying to say, and I know that he meant well, it was just the timing and the way of him saying it. What's funny is that sometimes when I say something half-ass and crazy, he would say to me, "If you don't say anything, nobody will know." Man I'll tell you..... men, I don't know what y'all be thinking sometimes, LOL.

## Tuesday, November 6, 2012 @ 10:05 PM

Hey Marcus, I have so many feelings and emotions right now. For the past couple of days now, I have been feeling like I want to adopt a little girl or become a foster mother. I've been thinking a lot about not being a grandmother. I have been feeling so sad inside about it. I can't ever write in this book without crying about it. There is a side of me that wants the love and attention, the kisses and hugs that you get from a little one. But there is a small side of me that thinks that I'm just trying to replace you. And you can never be replaced. I am just so lonely, so empty. Something is missing, and it's more than knowing that you're missing, I can't explain it.

What am I going to do Marc? I just hurt so much. Your trial is set for jury selection on March 11th. They said it's expected to last a week. And the trial begins March 18th and it's expected to last 3 weeks, but that's only if he pleads not guilty. I'm thinking about starting to take pills again, I think I need them.

## Monday, November 12, 2012 @ 4:30 AM

Hey Marc., I've only been up since about 3 a.m. flipping through TV channels. It's been over a year now, and I still keep waking up at this hour. I miss you so much. I am going to come see you later today. I miss you so much. I wish you could tell me why all this happened. I want you back so bad! I am so angry. How is it that someone can take someone's life and then act as if nothing happen? I want revenge Marc. I want these guys to pay for what they did to you. One gets 10 years for some crimes other than yours, one gets to basically walk, and the other MIGHT get life, but I doubt it. Marcus, what am I going to do?

## Sunday, December 9, 2012 @ 8:50 PM

I know that it's been just about a month since I last talked to you, in a way, I've been feeling like, if I don't face it, it's not real. I still feel like this is all a dream. I, for the most part stopped visiting you too. You know how I am; I tend to be overly dramatic. When I visit with you, I keep visually picturing you in that box. I picture you lying there, with that cloth over your face, with your hands crossed at your waist. I keep picturing how handsome you looked in your suite. I think about how you are only 6 feet below me. I just want to dig you up and touch you, I want to reach down and tell you to wake up, get up, Marcus get up. And then I stand there sometimes and think about what your body is going through, how your body is tearing down slowly, I gave birth to you, you grew inside me and now your body is breaking down slowly, what you must be going through hurts, angers and scares me. It's almost like I can actually see it happening, just only in slow motion, I don't know if you can understand what I'm trying to say. It's just that I know what is going to happen to your body over time, I can't get that image out of my head, I don't want that to happen. Then, I just stand there and look at the ground, and can't figure out why, why you, why me? Did this happen to me because I was a bad mother? That must be it because look at this, your gone, Nigel is in jail. What went wrong, what did I do wrong in raising the both of you? Am I that bad of a parent? I just keep thinking what I could have done differently in raising you both. I am so alone. I am so lonely, I am so lonely!

I just walked near your room and I smelled your cologne in the air. It was so strong, as if you were just standing there.

## Tuesday, December 18, 2012 @ 1:30 AM

Every day I think about how much of a good kid you are. I mean, you had your issues, kid issues, oh sorry, young adult issues, but you did not deserve this. I love you so much; I wish you would come back. I still have not been to see you, I just can't right now. I keep having those visions of seeing you in your coffin, just lying there. I keep imagining you waking up and saying "hey mom." Marcus do you even know why they did this to you? How well did or didn't you know these guys? Did that Emily girl you were dating have anything to do with this? Or did this have anything to do with that fight I hear that you were in a week or so before? I wish I had answers. Not that answers would make this any easier or help me, I just want to know more about what was going on in your life the last week or so of your life. We spoke that Wednesday before it happened, and you sounded happy, you were with Jamere and you talked to Nigel on the phone on 3-way. I just don't know.

07/19/2007

## Monday, December 31, 2012 @ 9:30 PM

Marcus, Jessica told me that she is pregnant. I have such conflicting feeling about it. On one hand, I am really, really happy for her. (FYI, I hope she has a girl) I'm happy for her, but at the same time it makes me mad, well not mad, maybe more sad than mad. While we were on the phone talking about her pregnancy, I felt…..mixed emotions. I mean, I want to be happy for her, but at the same time, it's just a reminder to me that you're not here. It's really hard to explain this to you. I'm hoping that she will allow me to be the babies God Mother, because when I talk to Jess, I feel your presence coming through her, I even get that feeling when I talk to Jamere and some of your other friends. I know how close you and Jess are, y'all considered each other family, and her mother and I grew up together, so maybe that is the closeness that I'm feeling from her. So why can't I be completely 100% happy for her. It's not that I don't want her to have a baby, it's just that I'm so caught up in my emotions of not having you here, that it's hard to be genuinely happy for someone else, I don't mean it! When she and I got off the phone, all I could do was cry, because this is something that you won't get to experience. All those years of me telling you and Nigel not to make me a grandmother, and now look! Her being pregnant makes me want to be a grandmother more than ever now, and I can't be. I am so angry that you didn't get the chance to experience fatherhood. OMG Marcus, just thinking about it makes me so damn angry! Every since she told me, I think about what your child might look like, how I would spoil her, and how much of a good father you would be. Woow Marc, you would be a great father. That is evident in how close you and Talia are, and how you treat your other younger nieces. It just hurts me that she is pregnant and you can't experience this. I love Jess, don't get me wrong, I just can't be fully happy for her knowing that you can't be a father, and I want to be a grandmother. But at the same time, I already feel close to the baby, because of you and Jess's relationship, crazy huh?

I told Nikki what I did, because I was feeling guilty. I told her that when Jess and I got off the phone, how I just cried and how I was upset over her being pregnant, but only because of you. You know what she said to me, she said "oh, well you must be still morning Marcus." What!! I can't believe that Nikki would say something like that to me. Like, is there a time limit on how long I'm supposed to morn my child! Really! But it just goes to show that unless you have experienced the loss of child, you don't really understand. But I guess she meant well, I think.

I think about what those stupid asses took from you, what they took from me! I can't believe that this has happened to you, I hate them so much!


**Tuesday, Jan 1, 2013 @ 12:40 PM**

Hey Marcus, well another year has passed without you in it, and I miss you so much. I thought about you all last night; how you would be out with your friends or over your Aunt Nikki's house. Then you would come home and sleep all day. But you know it angers me that people have gone on with their lives and you're not here to enjoy yours. I know that life goes on, but it's just so unfair. I wonder how many of your so-called friends even gave you a second thought. I have had a hard time going through my day to day activities without feeling some type of guilt, that if I have the least little bit of enjoyment that I'm wrong for it, because you are not here to enjoy and experience things for yourself. There were just a few, only a few people that posted on your Facebook page that they miss you and that they are thinking about you. No one called me.

Not much has really changed though; Nikki had her baby, which makes 4 girls for her now. Nigel is having a hard time. I know he thinks that I am not there for him. But I love and miss him just as much as you. Nigel is just so dead set on thinking that he can get out. Not to say that he should just settle, but when you are working with little to no money, there is only so much a person can do to help. I'm just tired. Sometimes I wish I could just close my eyes and not wake up. I got your trial coming up in March, Nigel keeps pulling me this way and that way, Garry, the Foundation, I'm lonely, it all might not seem like much to you, but I hate this feeling. But I guess some would say...such is life.

**Saturday, January 5, 2013 @ 10:25 PM**

Marcus, I miss seeing your face so much. You would think that I would be in a better place by now, but I'm not. Everything I want to do, personal or business, I want to or do in your honor, in your name.

I've been working on buying a house, and we are about to close on it, oddly, I'm not fully excited about it, because I wish that you were her to experience it with me. Why do I feel so sad and guilty about things?

**Wednesday, January 10, 2013 @ 3:20 AM**

Yesterday was Nigel's birthday, he turned 22. I went to go

see him; we had a really good visit. I wish he didn't have to spend it in prison. But it seemed to me that he had a pretty good attitude. I miss him so much and his bubbly attitude. Nigel could always make me laugh about something.

I finally told Nigel about Lionel Williamson, Kurt Dupree and Warren Brooks, although I wish I hadn't. I told him that Warren Brooks got out with no charges, well to me it was no charges, but with a 2 year conspiracy charge. Kurt Dupree only also got 2 years conspiracy, but he also got 10 years for other prior charges that was pending against him. I told him that both of them are going to testify at the trial against Lionel Williamson. I also told him that Kurt Dupree just got transferred to Smyrna from Georgetown. Sitting there telling him all of this, I could just see his mind spinning. He actually said to me that he was glad that he was locked up, because he would have went after them. He said that he probably would have been with you that night at the gas station. When I think about that, I could have lost both of you.

I was just thinking about how much you and Nigel would fuss and horse play in the house, all I would hear is "Marcus stop, stop Marcus, you play too much." I would start yelling at you to leave your brother alone and you would say, "Mom, its Nigel, he started it." Nigel would be laughing because you got yelled at. Marcus, I knew it was Nigel instigating it all along. Almost every day you and Nigel were fighting and arguing. As much as the two of you made me mad, I love how close the two of you are. The two of you were always together. I would do anything to have those days back again. You know that your court case is coming up in March. I'm not sure if I'm ready for it. I was watching the news yesterday morning and there was this 9 month old baby boy that was killed 2 years ago. The man that killed him was the next door neighbor, babysitting. The two families knew each other very well for the past 15 to 20 years the news said. The baby died, do to some type of burns on its body. The news said that after some time, the man admitted to pouring liquid drain-o on the baby while he was giving the baby a bath, just because the baby wouldn't stop crying. Marcus he admitted to what he did and he was only sentenced to 17 years. 17 years Marcus!! And he admitted to what he did. This really does not instill a lot of confidence in our legal system in me. If Lionel Williamson doesn't at least get life, Marcus I don't know what I'd do. I just don't know what I'd do.

## Friday, January 25, 2013 @ 9:30 AM

Marcus I had another dream last night that I either had a nervous breakdown, or I just went crazy. People kept coming into the house and going straight into your room and looking around. They would come in, walk past my room, and go into yours, sometimes they would come in and stand in front of my bedroom door and stare at me like they are taunting me. They would never say anything to me just stand there and look at me and then go into your room. I got up out of the bed to get these people out of the house, they were in your room just looking around, not taking anything, just looking around, almost like they were window shopping. I kept screaming from the top of my lungs for them to leave. It was like they were looking at me, but couldn't see me. You know how you could be looking at someone, but your mind is somewhere else, so you don't notice them? It was kind-of like that. So, they would be looking around your room and then they would leave, but someone else would come in right after them. I followed one of them out the house, and the front door was torn up. There was a big hole in the wall next to the door, the door frame was broken, so the door wouldn't close properly. But even with me standing there they were still coming in, walking right past me. They weren't going anywhere else in the house, just straight to your room, one after the other. The hole in the wall next to the door was so big that you could climb through it. But the door wouldn't close completely. I put my head through the hole to see what was on the other side, I saw a long line of people standing there waiting to come in. I ran into my room, laid on the bed in a ball, holding my legs, hiding my face between my knees and screaming. I just kept screaming for them to leave and to stop going into your room. None of them would talk to me and tell me why they were here. So I just kept screaming and screaming lying on the bed in a ball and rocking back and forth, crying. I don't know what bothered me the most about the dream, that people were in your room, or that I saw myself breaking down losing control.

Marcus, I think this is a sign that I shouldn't move back to Dover. I feel that I'll be leaving you behind here in this apartment. People are going to be moving in after I move out. I think that this is what it's all about.


## Sunday, February 3, 2013 @ 3:30 AM

I've been laying here tossing and turning since about 2:00, can't sleep. I went to bed about 11:00 pm, you would think that I'd be nice and tired, NOPE! Actually, I've been/still doing this again for a while now.

I was thinking, why is it that people regret that they

didn't tell the person they love how much they loved them. I know that our last words to each other the last time we talked was "I Love You." But I wish I had told you how much I am proud of you. You were becoming your own man. I so wish I had the chance to tell you that.

Your court case is next month. And I guess it's been on my mind a lot. I want to be there every day. But there is a side of me that thinks that I won't be able to handle it all. I want/have to be there to represent you. I have to be the one to speak for you, if I'm not there, then your voice won't be heard. I just keep getting this pain in my stomach like I want to throw up whenever I think about it. That might explain why I'm still waking up at this hour almost every night again.

## Thursday, February, 21, 2013 @ 8:00 PM

We had court today for Lionel Williamson, I think it was to hear testimony on whether to hold him over for trial. Marcus I am so fucking mad right now! I am so angry. I know that I shouldn't be, but this angers me so bad! I got a call from the AG's office yesterday, just yesterday, that he is going to be appearing in court today. I called, texted and talked to my family members and your friends about it, because from the start everybody was saying to make sure that I let them know when any court cases comes up so that they can be there. Everybody was always saying that they are going to be there to support me, represent you, whatever, just let them know when. I thought that this was going to be a very important case/ hearing. And so it was, but do you know that NO ONE showed up in court to represent you except me. NO ONE Marcus! Do you know how upsetting and lonely it was for me sitting there all by myself? Marcus no one was there, I was sitting there by myself. Marcus I had to sit there looking at him, acting like this is a fucking game, showing no remorse what-so-ever, they just don't know how painful that was for me, it hurt me to my core Marcus. He had about 8 or 10 people over there sitting on his side. People said that they would be there! They said that they were coming and that they would meet me at the courthouse. No one showed up! Marcus I am so heart broken and upset, I can't stop crying about it. I thought people loved you. People said to me all throughout this whole ordeal that they would be there to support me, no matter what! What happened?! I know that this hearing today was last minute, and I know that they have jobs, family and other things that they got to attend to, but they said that they were coming; they said that they would be here. They should not have said that they were coming if they were not sure about it. I expected people to show up. I sat there all by myself Marcus. I have no words for my family right now, fuck them, fuck them Marcus! I can't shake that feeling of sitting there all by myself with his family looking at me. I had to sit there holding back my tears; there was no one there for me to lean on. Marcus no one was there! Marcus, fuck my family, I can't believe that they weren't there. No family, no friends, no one! Ashlyn just texted me asking me how court went, I told her that I am so disgusted with everybody right now, and that I don't feel like talking to anyone. I don't blame her because I know that she is still in school, I know that she wasn't going to be there because of school, but everybody else. I'm not answering the phone if anyone calls, don't ask me shit! I really have no love for anyone right now! They just don't know how much they hurt me. Just leave me alone! Marcus I am hurting so bad right now, I can't stop crying, I'm sitting here on the floor holding my chest because it feels like my heart is about to explode, it just hurts so much. How could they do this to me? Marcus I sat there in that court room wondering if anyone was going to show up, and no one did. All they had to say was that it was too last minute for them, but they said that they were coming.

I just can't believe that no one was there. NO ONE, NO ONE, NO ONE! I know I said this before but it's just so fucked up. It's just that when you passed, like for the first couple of months or so, everybody was so concerned about how this was going to affect Nigel. Everybody said we are going to make a visit and go see Nigel. Everybody said that they want to make sure that he's going to be ok, they want to know how he's dealing. And this is my family saying this. Guess how many or who has gone to see him so far? NO ONE! I just can't swallow this Marc. No one showed up in court today. I feel so deserted and abandoned. I sat there with no one beside me. How can my family do this to me? I am so emotional over the fact that no one was in court with me, that I can't even remember what happen or what was said. He had so many people sitting over there on his side, and you know that we have to sit on separate sides of the court room. No one was on my side! I feel so alone right now, I feel like screaming! I don't think that I want to tell anyone else again about what's going on with the case. How could they do this to me? How could they just not show up after telling me that they would? How could they just leave me alone like that? Marcus if I had any hate in my heart right now, it would be for them! I am truly hurt Marcus. I want to excuse them for it because I know that it was last minute, but they still said that they would be there. It's just that my heart hurts right now, I am so sad, angry and discouraged about all this, it's as if no one cares.

What am I going to do Marcus? From both your court case today, and people saying that they were worried about Nigel, I should be used to broken promises by now.

## Friday, February 22, 2013 @ 7:15 PM

Guess what Marcus, we closed on the house in Dover today, we are officially homeowners! So truly excited, but yet still exhausted from yesterday.

## Thursday, March 7, 2013 @ 8:15 PM

Guess what Marcus? Through his lawyer, Lionel Williamson took a plea and pled guilty today to: Murder Second Degree and Possession of a Firearm During the Commission of a Felony. I went into the AG's office today so that they could explain the next steps. They have scheduled the sentencing hearing for May 15th. The court is doing what they call a Presentencing Investigation on both our families. I have to go into the investigators office and talk to them about how your death has affected me, talk to them about the type of person you are. Nikki is going to go with me. This guilty plea comes after a testimony given by Kurt Dupree, who finally is talking about what happen that night, who said what, who did what. They allowed Lionel Williamson to hear the testimony that Kurt Dupree gave, and after hearing that, he plead guilty and took a plea bargain. So there is not going to be a jury trial, the judge is going to hear the case, and sentence him. So after the judge hears the case, it will be a matter of how much time the judge decides to give him. I'm hoping for the best (a long sentence), but expecting the worst.

## Saturday, March 9, 2013 @ 11:45 PM

Happy Birthday Marcus. I went to see you today, and put balloons and fresh flowers on you. You made the wind blow again, telling me that you were there. I miss you so much! Jessica and Adrian went to go see you too. But we weren't together though; we all went at different times.

Marcus I don't know if I have already told you this but, a few of your family members and friends all got tattoos of the Smiley faces, or some variation of a Smiley face that represents you, since your nick name was Smiley. I think that is one of the most affectionate and ultimate ways someone can show love, respect and appreciation for someone. Some of the tats are so elaborate and beautiful. You must have meant so much to them. I love looking at them. I want to get one of you on my back near my neck of your face. But I just got to find the right person to do it. It has to be someone who is good at drawling portrait tattoos. Because if it doesn't come out right, I am going to be pissed! So I will wait to get mine until I find the right place/person to do it.

## Wednesday, May 8, 2013 @ 9:50 AM

Hey Marcus, I miss you so much. Things are just not the same without you. I know I have not talked to you in a while, at least not here in my journal to you. And so much has happened. I don't know where to begin. Well, you know that Larry, Nigel's dad died last week on May 2nd. I didn't want to tell Nigel at first because I didn't know how he would take it. He was transferred to Georgetown C.I. and was put in the hole because he fought his transfer from Smyrna to Georgetown. He didn't want to go to Georgetown because he thought that Lionel Williamson was still there. But he had already been transferred to Gander Hill in Wilmington, we just didn't know about it (I'll tell you more about that later). Anyway, I was supposed to be told of any moves he makes by the VINE system, but they didn't notify me of this one. Anyway, the sentencing hearing for Lionel Williamson is next week on the 15th, There is a big side of me that's not ready to face it. I almost feel like not even showing up. I walk around like everything is ok with me. I don't really talk about it all that much, don't think anyone really cares anyway. I just don't feel up to having him or his family looking at me.

A few weeks ago I had a dream; yes Marcus, another dream, lol. I kept falling off a cliff, there was nothing happening in the dream that lead up to me being on a cliff. The scene kept starting with me at the cliff, like a waterfall, and I was standing at the edge of the cliff, looking down, but I had to lean over to get a clear view, but as I leaned over, I just kept going over the edge. I didn't hesitate or try to fight the fall by trying to stop myself from falling or trying to catch myself, I mean I didn't act as if I was scared of going over the cliff, I just kept going. And that scene just kept playing over and over again; it kept repeating itself, me falling over a cliff. I think that dream is a sign of me losing control.

As you know, we moved back to Dover, I put a key for you outside the front door in the flower bed, in the dirt. That key is there for you anytime you are ready to come home. I wish I could be there with you to know how you are doing, but Nigel needs me here. If I leave, Nigel won't have anyone to count on. And I won't do that to him. But I know that you need me too!

Oh, Oh, Oh, I know all about that fight you and your cousin were in at Smithers. Remember I told you a while ago that his kids were in our youth golf program last summer, and we stopped the program because of it? Well guess what? This is some crazy shit here; he lives right next door to us. Right Next Door! Not across the street, not 2 or 3 doors down, RIGHT NEXT DOOR! You know our house is a twin, so it's just our two houses that are connected together. We share a driveway, that kind of next door, next door. Marcus my heart hit the floor when I found out. How I found out is just as crazy. Nikki came over one day, before she came into the house, I could hear her outside talking to someone about insurance. When I got to the door to open it for her, I heard her telling someone, that they could get her cell phone number from me. I didn't pay it any mind who she was talking to; I just thought it was someone she knew. So, when she comes into the house, she says hey, that guy next door I think he is so-n-so's brother. She said, you know how when you see someone you know and you know that you know them, but you just can't put a name to the face? She just couldn't remember his name. So about two days later, I was coming home, when I got out of the car this guy started talking to me from his up stair window, he said to me, "excuse me, I talked to your sister the other day when she was here, and she said that I could get her phone number from you." Now I do remember hearing Nikki telling someone to get her number from me, so because I heard that, I went on and gave him her cell phone number. Nikki calls me later that night to tell me who it was. She said that someone had called her cell number but she didn't answer the phone because she didn't recognize the number, you know how we do, lol. So they texted her, it said: "Hey this is so-n-so, I got your number from your sister." Now the rest of that text was about whatever they talked about outside the house, but it also reminded her of who she was talking to or who she thought she was talking to at my house that day and that it wasn't the person who she thought it was. It was actually him, not his brother! She called me right away to tell me who I was living next to. Marcus, the word on the street is that this is the person who put a hit out on you. The word on the street is that he sent those boys to do what they did. This comes from a source of Nikki's. But of course people want to stay anonymous about things they know. Now I heard it said from a different person that this person is a known drug dealer. I'm hearing that he is claiming to be the HNIC of the bloods, so I'm hearing.

Marcus, I want so badly to go over there and ask him why? Why did you do this to my son? I want to go over there and put my fist in his face. Marcus what are the freaking chances that I would move right next door to him. If this situation was the lottery, I'd be rich. But I'm trying to stay strong about it. But I have to admit too, I am just a little scared, no, I am scared. Because you don't know what people's motives are. Who's to say that he doesn't want to get back by using the whole family? We don't know what the cause or the reason is for him doing what he did. People do crazy things for stupid reasons. Honestly, I feel like a prisoner in my own house. And if he is the type of person that I'm hearing he is, everything that he is involved in, then I have every right to be scared, especially because I don't know the real reason why he did it.

Based on source, Nikki's take on this whole thing is that it was all about jealousy. She said that she thinks that it stemmed from that fight that you and your cousin were in a week or so prior to that night at Smithers. It was something about your cousin was speaking to some girl, "he" didn't like it, your cousin and "him" had words and got into it, other people got in it, you jumped in it, and-so-on. Nikki thinks, that because a person of your age, 22, who is riding around in a nice car, that people might have been a little jealous, she said that there are people a lot older than you who don't have what you have, and they be hating on you. But again, she doesn't know for sure what the fight was really about that night, she is just speculating. But hearing that people being jealous over you is not the first time that I heard that. Jamere said the same thing too. But whatever the motives Marcus, you didn't deserve this. And whether or not "he" did have something to do with this, it's just enough for me that he was even questioned about it at all.

### Sunday, May 12, 2013 @ 2:15 PM

I spent the day with you today. I know you knew I was there because as usual, the wind blew. I know it was you saying hello. I was just a little mad, because the last time I was there the grass had not been cut, and the weeds and grass around your headstone was high, so this time I brought my weed whacker and spruced up a little bit, I know people was looking at me like I was crazy, but I don't care.

I went to Nigel's dad, Larry's funeral yesterday (I'm going to miss him). I don't know if they allowed Nigel to go. I don't think that they did. Marcus I feel so sorry for him, the Chaplain from the prison called me, he also said that he is concerned for Nigel. Nigel feels that everybody is leaving him. First you, then my mom, and now his dad. I can't blame him for feeling that way. He is scared that something is going to happen to me before he gets out. Honestly Marcus, I feel the same way. He feels that he won't have anybody when get gets out. Nobody in the family is even reaching out to him. Although after you left, everybody kept asking about how his was doing, that they were going to go see him, and support him. Make sure that he's ok, but all that concern fizzled out. He said he gets a letter every blue moon, but that I am about the only person that writes to him, and that's because I'm his mother. I don't know what to tell him. At the funeral, people asked how he was doing, but that's about all. It just makes me think, if it's not your own, why should anyone care? Shame.

Let me tell you something that I know you don't know, and neither did I up until now. Well, Warren Brooks, the one who is out right now, well I just found out who his mother is. Our families are very well known to each other, very well known. Our families used to hang out together when they were younger. We all went to the same church. (When I say "we" I mean my older brothers, I wasn't born yet, but I still grew up knowing who they were) Your uncles, Butch, Roy, Poppy, Chris, they all went to high school together. We use to be neighbor's! We went to their house as kids, and them ours. Our families knew each other so well that, your Uncle Poppy has Warren Brooks mom on video tape from when they used to hand out together when they were younger. But get this, I found out or rather, I was informed about who she was on Saturday at Larry's funeral. There were some people there that I knew from a long time ago. They were basically asking me how I was doing and we did talk briefly about the case, and one conversation lead to another and it just came out who his mother was. But the way it came out, it was like they knew that I should know who his mother was. It was like the way that they were responding was like they were surprised that I didn't know who she was, they were acting like I should know who they were talking about. So after a little bit of us talking back and forth, they said her last name, her maiden name. I was like "wait a minute," you mean to tell me that his mother is so-and-so? I know her, I know her family. Marcus I stood there like Woooow! It set me back a little. I remember going to a church outing to Bush Gardens when I was young with his uncle. We rode the Loch Ness Monster Roller Coaster together. I remember that like it was yesterday, he said that I could sit next to him if I promise not to scream. Marc I had to be like only 12, I think, wow!  A whole year has gone by, and I am just finding this out. Your Uncle Darryl already knew this information, but he said that he didn't say anything to me about it because he thought that I already knew, he told me that he saw Warren Brooks mother in Wal-Mart one day, and she acted like and looked at him as if she didn't know him. Darryl is Facebook friends with his uncle, and up until you left, Darryl said that they used to communicate back and forth to each other on FB and then it all stopped, I guess when they found out that you were my son. But I don't think that they knew right off that I was your mother, because I think that they know me by Schatze and not by Joreen, and you are

Ware and I am Sykes. Or maybe they did, because they spoke about your case in the Delaware State Newspaper a few times, they interviewed me a few times too.

I see on the police report that his mother or he lives in Magnolia. I want to go talk to her to find out what she knows, I still feel like I need answers. You know people don't understand why I have this strong desire to want to know why, I just need to know. Not that I would expect that his mother would know or have any answers, I just feel like I need to ask, I want to know what ever she knows. I don't know why I even continue to discuss with others my feeling about that, they are not ever going to understand. I have a need to know why this happened to you. I don't care that it's not going to change anything. I mean I do care, I just know that it's not going to change anything that happened to you. Until they have lost a child, they will never understand. I feel like people just want me to sit back and just accepted what happen to you. 'Oh ok, your son is gone now, ok, you've cried, now just get over it". I'm not going to do that! I am your voice; I am here to speak for you now. Because everybody else chose to move on, everybody else is silent now, I won't be!

I woke up this morning feeling worst then yesterday. Today I feel like I want to faint, kind-of like I just want to pass out. I have no motivation, no energy. I'm not looking forward to Wednesday at all. Something in my heart tells me that Lionel Williamson along with the other two is not going to get anything but a slap on the hand. I'm nervous about going, I just know, I just know that he is going to get a light sentence.

## Monday, May 13, 2013 @ 2:40 AM

Marcus, I am feeling so scared right now. I don't know what is going to happen Wednesday. I just have this strong feeling that it's not going to be good. I want justice for you. I mean it will never be justice. I have a feeling that the judge is only going to give him 25 years which means he'll probably be out in 18 to 20. The judge does have the option to give him more years, but I don't think he will.

I had to go to the AG's office today, they allowed me listen to Kurt Dupree's new testimony. Actually, I don't think that they can really consider it a testimony because he has already been tried and convicted of the crime. Sgt. Spicer said that they just went there on a whim to see if he had anything else to add or share, he didn't know that they were coming. Kurt Dupree talked about how they were at the same party that you were at that night in Camden. They went to Dover Downs after the party, and later they ended up at the same gas station that you were at. In a nut shell, he just basically said that while at the gas station Lionel Williamson pointed you out to him as "that boy" who he had told him about that he had a conflict with a year ago. Now if he's the type of person that shoots someone over an argument that happen over a year ago, then he needs to be behind bars. Anyway, I think he did say that he admitted to knowing what was going to happen once at the gas station. He talked about how Warren Brooks reached under the seat and handed Lionel Williamson the gun, pushing, encouraging him, and tell him that if he is going to do it, then he needs to do it now. Proving that they all had knowledge. He talked about how Lionel Williamson got out of the car, went behind the gas station but came back and got back in the car because he said that someone was back there taking a piss. But Kurt Dupree's new testimony doesn't do much for the case now, so after listening to Kurt Dupree's new testimony, Lionel Williamson took the plea bargain but both Kurt Dupree and Warren Brooks have already received their sentences, you can't charge a person twice for the same crime. And we are just two days away from Lionel Williamson final trial. Kurt Dupree's testimony described everything on the surveillance video from that night, almost exactly to detail. Why he chose to give this new testimony now, late, I don't know, he just did. Kurt Dupree admitted to everything that he took part in, that he was the driver, that he drove with the head lights off. He also did say that there was a 4th person in the car but he didn't know who it was. Too little to late is all that I have to say Marc. Why wasn't he so willing to give up all this information before?

**Tuesday, May 14, 2013 @ 8:55 PM**

Tomorrow's the day Marcus. I can't do this. My chest hurts, my stomach is turning. I was feeling so bad last night. I tried so hard not to think about it. I took my meds in the afternoon. I felt like I slept the whole day away. I just woke up and still feel the same. I don't know who is going to show up to court tomorrow, family, friends, I don't know. At this point I guess it doesn't really matter. Like I always felt...if I don't support my kids, who will?

**Wednesday, May 15, 2013 @ 4:15 pm**

Well Marcus, it's all over. They sentenced him to 45 years. After they do all the math, adding up time served and good behavior, and all that other crap they use to reduce sentences, it winds up being 33 years with a mandatory of 20. It's just what I thought Marc, I said 25 years and he gets 20. He has to do 20 years before they will consider him for release. That's all your life is worth to them.

Marcus they made Lionel Williamson look like he was the victim. We were in court for over 3 hours, 2 of those hours seemed like it was just hearing testimony to Lionel Williamsons' character. They talked about his upbringing, about how he was raised; with having no a real male figure in his life was cause for him doing what he did. Because he had no real structure in his life, he didn't have a stable family life, is why he was in and out of jail. I mean it seemed like we went to court to hear why we should be giving the boy a second chance, why he should have a light sentence. Not because he took a life. I mean Marcus, it just went on and on about him. They spoke nothing to your character, the type of person you were or anything. I think they should have, you are a person, a living breathing person. You are somebody's son, brother, friend. I really felt like the case wasn't about you anymore, it was about him. Spare him, let's show concern and sympathy about him and all that he's been through, he's a troubled person with issues. Shut the Fuck Up!

In the court room, the defense gave his whole life story starting from age 4. It was so long and drawn out. I thought we were watching a soap opera. I could see your attorney Dave Favata getting irritated, the expressions on his face was funny and priceless. They said that his reason for taking your life was a result of some damn argument that happen over a year ago. A Year Ago Marcus….Really?! You are far more a better person then he is, and even though he is about 5 or 6 years older than you, he wasn't man enough to deal with you being a better person, and that's why he took your life! They also brought up Emily's name, I don't know why, but I want to know. We always felt that she may have had something to do with it. I know that Jessica said that Emily was fooling around with Lionel Williamson. I've heard a lot of bad negative things about her. I never really liked her, how she dressed or anything, she dressed hoochie. So I am real interested to know why they brought her name up in court. I also thought that you should know that Jamere was there for you in court too! Your Uncles Butch, and Poppy was there, Ashlyn; Kenya; Mr. Garry; Ki-Ki, and her nephew Will, Diane Glenn and Sgt. Spicer were there. If anyone else was there, I didn't notice them, they might have been sitting behind me.

When he was given the opportunity to speak, he briefly looked back at me and I started crying harder, he said that he was sorry for what he did and he hopes that me and my family will be able to forgive him, is he for real?! Is he kidding me? He killed my son. I can't and won't find forgiveness in that. Is he fucking joking!? A part of his testimony was that he didn't mean to kill Marcus, that he was only trying to scare him. Wow, my thing is with that Marcus, is that in the meeting that we had the other day with the attorneys, they were again explaining to me why they had to go with the charges that they went with, because they couldn't prove that Lionel Williamson intended to kill Marcus. Now, if your attorneys are telling me this, don't you think that his attorneys are saying the same thing to him, using that same strategy? That to go with the defense that you didn't mean to kill him, by saying that you were only trying to scare him. But how can you scare someone about something if they don't know what's going on? My thing about that Marc is that he got out of the car twice, twice! The first time he said he came back because someone was behind the gas station taking a piss, so he goes back again! I'm sorry, for me, that shows intent. I just don't see it any other kind of way! He shot you in the back, in the back Marcus, while you were trying to get a jump for your car. I can see him using that defense that he was only trying to scare you, only if you actually knew what was about to happen. If he was only trying to scare you, why didn't he get your attention and then shoot in the air?  I can't remember all that was said in court, I wonder if I can get a transcript of the hearing?

Marcus I was so emotional I was shaking, I am still shaking. After all the BS was done with him, I had to read my impact statement. Marcus I know that I said that I am your voice, but I just couldn't do it. I am so sorry, I couldn't get up, my feet just wouldn't move, all I could do was cry on Garry's shoulder. So Dave Favata, your attorney read the impact statement for me. I wasn't watching but I could hear, he did a great job reading it, he read it the exact same way that I was feeling it when I wrote it. I couldn't have done a better job reading, and even though it was my words, he read it better than I would have.

**Impact Statement:**

*The first thing that I need to say is that Lionel Williamson is a coward!*

*I don't know how to begin or know what to say. Horror, agony, emptiness, chaos, confusion and hopelessness are my more present feelings. But these words seem only trite in describing what followed when I lost my son to murder. However, words cannot truly express the pain and anguish I'm feeling. To articulate the impact that Marcus's death has had on me is truly overwhelming and impossible.  All*

*I can think about is that there will be no more birthdays, backyard gatherings, holidays or other activities for us to share as a family.  His laughter, hugs, his smile, and the opportunities to say I love you just once more are gone. My heart is so broken. My heart aches for my son so badly.*

*I'm mourning the loss of so many hopes, dreams and expectations.  Because of Warren's selfish careless decision to pick up a gun and shoot my son cowardly in the back, my younger son now assumes the role of being an only child, a role that is unfamiliar and unfair to him.*

*Judge, you don't know my son Marcus, the coward sitting here to my left who willingly shot my son didn't know him either, because to know Marcus is to love Marcus.  Marcus was born on March 9, 1989 at 10:36 in the morning, he was handsome, Marcus was so handsome. There was no guessing if he was a boy or a girl, you know just by looking at him. Marcus grew to be tall, slim, reserved, smart and loved to draw.  He was respectful. Marcus loved his younger brother and younger cousins. I remember once his little cousin was a flower girl in a wedding, she was about 6 or 7 years old, when it was her turn to walk down the aisle, she cried and had a fit yelling for Marcus. She wanted her cousin Marcus to walk with her.*

*Marcus is my first born; He did not deserve to be so cruelly taken.*

*There are no adequate words to describe the immense pain, anger and despair that I have endured over this past 18 months. The pain I feel hurts me to my core. I never thought I would be without my child in this manner.*

*Every day I sit in an empty home, a home that Marcus*

*used to come and call home. A home where his friends would come over and spend time. A place where him and his brother would always fight and play. Me yelling at the both of them to stop wrestling on the couch. One child getting mad because I punished him and not the other, then one teasing the other for it. But now I have trouble finding joy in the simple pleasures. Why do I now have to resort to only a memory? This is not fair. Being happy doesn't seem right anymore for me. Sometimes the feeling of despair becomes so over whelming so oppressive, that I literally can't function. I never know what sight, sound or smell or anything will trigger memory of him. With my memories, comes the realization that he is gone, and it's devastating.*

*Marcus was killed somewhere between the hours of 2:30 and 3am, and since that night, for days, weeks, and months I continuously  wake up at that exact time. No matter what time that night I go to sleep, I just wake up. I try to stay a sleep. Meds don't help me; going to bed late doesn't help me, nothing! This has truly by all means taken a physical and emotional toll on me.*

*Never in my life, have I felt or have had so much hate in my heart for anyone. I hate Lionel Williamson, he is a coward. My life has been impacted at such a magnitude that I will never be the same again.*

*Lionel Williamson not only took my sons life, the life that I gave to him, but he took away his brothers only sibling.  He took away any chance for Marcus to be a great father; he took away any possibility of Marcus being called uncle. He deprived me of being a grandmother. I want so badly to be a grandmother.*

*The defendant will do his time in jail, and someday get out, be a so-called father to his children, and be able to walk around and act as if this has never happened, and probably commit this crime again. But what about me? What about the children Marcus will never have? What about his brother, his family and friends that are left here with only memories. Marcus will never walk this earth again, never to be seen or heard again. Having pictures is fine, but it's not enough, I am his mother, he is supposed to be here with me, talking, laughing, and smiling. I am supposed to be watching him right now, being and growing into a magnificent man, husband and father that I know he could have been.*

*I cannot express enough how much it angers me that one day I may see Lionel Williamson walking down the street. Just thinking about that makes me want to scream and pull my hair out. My son is gone, my son is gone. It's like a tape recorder playing over and over in my head, and I want it to stop. Sometimes, it's still unreal to me that I have to resort to going to a cemetery to visit with my child. This is unreal. I just can't believe that this is my life now.*

*We live by a law in this country so that, ideally, no one will ever have to know what it is like to be a victim of such a violent crime. If I had my wish, it would be that no one ever again would have to go through what I am going through today, and endure for the rest of my life. Crimes such as this are intolerable. The law recognizes this and it provides for punishment that will ensure at least, that others will not suffer again at the same hands. I pray that this is true today.*

*The defendant is taking this plea today, not because he is truly admitting guilt for what he did, he's given no reason why, he is ONLY taking this plea because he feels it's the easiest and quickest way for him to get away with what he did. He is not sorry for what he did, he may say that he's sorry just to appease the court, but he says this because he thinks that he is only going to get a slap on the hand and told not to do this again.*

*Lionel Williamson handed my son a death sentence and me a life sentence. He needs to be taught a lesson; he needs to be made an example of for future criminals. His actions are not acceptable in the eyes and hearts of us who have lost someone at the hands of others. He needs to be shown that we cannot put a number on someone's life, a life that did not belong to him. Why should the court show this coward any pity or mercy, he did not show Marcus any. I believe that the punishment should fit the crime, but I also believe in an eye for an eye. He should be punished for all the things that he took from Marcus, and for all the things that he took from me, and what he took from me was someone who is a better man then he could ever hope to be.*

*It is my belief that anyone who knowingly and deliberately picks up a hand gun, hides and covers up his face, to creep and make the insane decision to take the life of another, to take the life of my son Marcus, and without any conscious, remorse or reason, should suffer the same fate, or at the least, be locked up for life. To shoot a person, an unarmed; unsuspecting person is just inconceivable to me. So that the defendant might one day understand the magnitude of the losses he inflicted on us the night of Oct 8, 2011, it is my request that the maximum penalty be imposed on him for the crime he committed not only against Marcus, but a crime against his only sibling Nigel, a crime against his family and friends and a crime against me.*

After I got home from the sentencing, I sat down on the couch, I let out a big breath, it was like you were telling me to breathe. I felt lighter, like a heavy weight had been lifted off of me. I feel relieved that it's all over with now. I mean Marcus, I'm upset at the outcome, I just don't have to go to the courts or the hearings anymore. I still have questions that need answers, I still kind-of feel like it's not over yet, but yet, it's over. It's hard to explain what I'm feeling right now.

One thing that I didn't like about the court system Marcus, is why didn't I have some say or some type of influence as to the outcome. Decisions are made in whose best interest? Not mine, and certainly not yours! I mean you are the one that a crime was committed against, but I am also, a crime was committed against me too. I was not asked or consulted with, I was told or informed that this or that was going to happen or we offered x,y,z plea to the offender. I mean, I know that I would not have been able to make real decisions about your case, I know that the law is the law and it's written a certain way, but how are they able to negotiate on your behalf? They didn't even know you! I feel that in a case like yours, that the family should have some bearing on the outcome. What the family wants should be a part of the negotiations. We should not just be told what offers are on the table. I am a victim too. I know that some families would probably say, give him the chair, or he should never see the light of day again; give him life in prison without ever getting out. I just think that some request should be taken into consideration, within reason. I would have asked that Lionel Williamson do a minimum mandatory of 35 to 40 years before he would be considered for release, not after only doing 20 years, like I always said, these sentencing's are weak.

## Thursday, May 16, 2013 @ 6:20 PM

Hey Marcus, I was in Walmart today, I was picking up a card for your attorneys' just to say thank you for their service on your trial. While I was there picking out a card this girl walked up to me and asked me if she could give me a hug. I didn't know who she was, but she said that she saw me in court yesterday. She said I'm sorry for your loss, hugged me, and walked away. I appreciated the sentiment and all, but it bothers me that people I don't know, who knows about us or your case, knows me, or recognizes me, but I don't know them. It makes me feel like not wanting to leave the house.

## Friday, May 17, 2013 @ 3:30 PM

I wish I knew how you feel about the sentencing. How do you put a number on someone's life? I just can't get over that when he gets out, you will still be gone. How is that justice? In the newspaper the next day, Williamson's family (his mom) made statements and also sent a message to me giving me their condolences, and they hope that one day I will be able to forgive their son. They also said how can I say in my impact statement, that I hate Lionel Williamson, when my foundation is supposed to represent just the opposite. I wrote his mom a letter, but I'm not sure if I'm going to mail it to her. Even if I don't send it to her, at least I got it off my chest. And besides, I'm angry right now, I don't want to send it in anger, so maybe I'll just wait a while before I do. But then again, why should I be considerate of someone else's feelings, no one was towards mine. I told her exactly how I felt and why I hate her son. And that I have every reason to feel this way. She said in the paper, that what if the shoe was on the other foot. So I threw that comment right back at her, what if the shoe was on the other foot? What would you do, how would you feel, what would you say? I asked her if she went to go visit you at the cemetery. NO! Why not, cause it's not her son that's lying there, It's mine. I said a lot of things to her. But I never sent her the letter, but just writing it down got it off my chest.

## My Letter To The Williamson Family:

*Ms. Williamson & family,*

*I wanted to respond to the comments you made to me in the Delaware State Newspaper.*

*It is truly unfortunate that either of us have to go through this. And this is the purpose of my foundation! Not to see another child or parent experience the misfortunes that I have to endure. I don't want another parent to have to experience the pain of burying their child or having them locked up behind bars for however many of years. People are going to feel the way that they feel, regardless. We are not saying that you shouldn't be angry or mad about a situation, but how you handle those emotions, what you do with those emotions is the root of what we are trying to get to. You can scream and holler all you want, but nothing should result in violence, whether it be physical or verbal attacks. My son's foundation is about teaching and showing our youth ways to recognize and handle aggression and confrontations, without the use of violence, something that your son Lionel didn't show towards my son. And you are right, the shoe could have been on the other foot, I am fully aware that this could be you writing me this letter, but the fact stands, it's not, it's my foot the shoe is on.*

*The statement I made in my impact statement that I hate Lionel Williamson, is where my heart lies. Foundation or not, I have every right to feel this way. The fact stands that he shot and killed my son, for whatever the reason, was it worth taking someone's life? How can you expect someone... me, to forgive that? Does his reasons really justify the end result? What happened to the old time fist fights?*

*There was a lot of talk in the court room as to who said what, and who did what, but at the end of the day, it is my son, Marcus who is gone! They spoke a lot about events that led up to that night, but Marcus is the one who is not here to defend himself or to say what happened". I find it curious that everything the defense said that supposedly led up to that night, the argument and fighting at the museum, the car chasing and cars with bullet holes, his family member getting shot in the arm, why wasn't any of this documented? There are no police reports of any of that happening, or my sons' involvement in it. Why? We have one statement, one side of the story, and one person dead! This is why I feel the way that I do towards your son. Now, until the day when Marcus can come back and say "mom, it wasn't entirely his fault, I didn't or maybe had some part in it", to me, which is unlikely that he would say that, am I to believe that what your son is saying is 100%? HELL NO! I don't think so! Let me ask you, if the shoe WAS on the other foot, how would you feel? Would you just accept it for what it is? Would it be easy for you to forgive? Have you gone to the cemetery to visit with Marcus? NO! Why? Because he's not YOUR son! Lionel asked for special provision for him to be moved to Smyrna prison for you and his family, so that it makes it easier for you to visit with him while I am relegated to visiting my son in a cemetery. You commented in the paper that I have memories of*

Marcus's life; do you really think that is enough? Do you really think that memories are what I want? I want my son, here; living; breathing; laughing! How can you truly compare my memories to yourself? How can you say that you have suffered a tremendous loss, your son will one day get to come home and act as if nothing has happened; he gets to have his life. In 20 plus years, Marcus will still be gone, how does this begin to bring me relief.

Lionel acts remorseful, but again, at the end of the day, my son is gone. I do hope that this does provide an opportunity for change in your son and in our society. Let this be a lesson that the choices we make and the people we choose as friends can lead to bad decisions and have severe consequences.

Not to diminish the experience or sorrow that you may be going through, but I believe I have endured much more than you. It's not just at the fact that my son is gone; it's also other things that have occurred since my son's passing, like being exploited for money by someone who said that Marcus was the father of her little girl, which turned out to be false.

The defense attorney painted Lionel to be a victim of his upbringing. In listening to his situation, you and I are not that much different. I too was a single mother of two kids; I too, moved around a lot, I too had to hold down countless jobs. Marcus never knew his father, he died when he was 2 years old in a car crash, but still he did have positive male role models in his life. One major difference between you and I, comes in where I have never been married; but I too have found love from time-to-time. But Marcus did not get involved in the same type of activity as your son. So using his upbringing was *just an easy excuse. Marcus has a high school diploma, Marcus worked for a company for 3 ½ years up to his death, that he started working for at the age of 18. Marcus has never been arrested for any illegal activities guns; drug;, robberies or otherwise. Lionel has had the opportunity to have children. Marcus has not. You are a grandmother, I am not., how do I beging to forgive that?*

*Lionel said that he regrets and accepts full responsibility for what he did. Given his background and the opportunities he's had to change, I can only hope and pray that he truly means it. It saddens me that people can't appreciate how precious life is and how fragile the human body is until after the fact.  Too many times a crime is committed, and then when it's time for court and sentencing, now they want forgiveness or they've found Jesus and see the error of their ways, and now all of a sudden they want the court to give and have leniency on them.*

*I don't know if maybe one day I will be able to accept Lionel's apology and forgive him, only time will tell.  My pain runs deep. I don't know, maybe one day I would want to sit down and talk to Lionel about all that has happened, maybe one day, Lionel will say where the gun is or what he did with the gun that he used to kill my son. I still have unanswered questions. Maybe one day Lionel and I will be able to talk and form some kind of understanding, I don't know.*

*But for now, as a mother who has lost her child, I am entitled to feel anyway that I choose, and grieve for as long as I need to. Now, like I said at the beginning, it is unfortunate that both of us have to experience this. This is a sad situation for any family, but….at the end of the day, Marcus is gone forever, and for this, I hate Lionel Williamson! Ms. Sykes*

I'm sitting here at Silver Lake Park right now as I'm talking to you. It's so peaceful right now, the weather is very nice, it's not too hot, it's about 75 to 80 degrees out. I remember back in the day, this park was the spot. Everybody came through. But you wouldn't know anything about that; you still a young buck.

I have not felt like sitting in the house since court. I just don't want to be there alone. I feel like I need to get away, if only for a couple of days. But I also must say that on Thursday after I wrote that letter to his family, there was a feeling of calm that came over me. I'm still angry, but I'm also relieved that the whole thing, the court process is over. What's next?

I found out yesterday that they did not let Nigel go to his dads' funeral. They didn't let him go to your funeral and now, not even his own dad. I feel so sad for him. He feels like everybody is leaving him and no one is going to be here when he gets out. I hope that his family on Larry's sides really reaches out to him now.

You know Marcus, its days like this that makes me shake my head in disbelief, it's just so unreal that you are not here. It's so beautiful out today, I know what you would be out doing...cleaning your car and blasting your music, I can just see you now. And I know that you would have probably taken some of my household cleaning supplies to clean your car, like my Windex window cleaner, that you always say that you don't have, I see you smiling right now 'cause you know I'm right, it's not funny.

## Saturday, May 25, 2013 @ 9:55 PM

First things first, Warren Brooks was arrested yesterday. The newspaper said that there was a month long investigation and he along with two others were arrested on drug, gun charges, resisting arrest and other things. (Dave Spicer told me not to believe everything that I read in the paper) I hope this time that fool stays in jail! I was so excited when I read that in the newspaper. Marcus even thought I knew it had nothing to do with your case; just the thought of him being back in jail makes me feel relieved. But I got to admit, I was jumping up and down in excitement when I read it in the newspaper.

## Thursday, May 30, 2013 @ 5:05 AM

Marcus I feel like I'm on an emotional overload. I miss you so much. I wish you'd come back. I can't say enough how much I miss seeing you and hearing your voice. I am so lonely, I hate being in the house by myself without you and Nigel.

I got some of your property back from the police that they had from that night that they were holding as evidence. They had your cloths, wallet, and shoes. I had previously gotten back your keys. All that I asked to get back was your wallet and the shoes you had on.

I didn't want your cloths back; I thought that might be too much for me to have.....emotionally. Wow Marcus, out of all the nice pairs of sneakers you have, you have about 25 pairs of high-end sneakers, you chose to have these beat-up red things on, LOL. But I know that was your style, you had a style that was all your own. I carry your wallet with me in my purse. I'm going to keep it with me at all times, promise. Marcus, I couldn't help but notice that the AAA roadside assistance card is in your wallet, so I have to ask you, why didn't you use it that night? Why?

## Monday, June 17, 2013 @ 9:30 AM

Marcus, I knew Nigel has been holding back some really emotional feelings, but I didn't know it was like this! Well actually, I kind-of-knew that he might want revenge. But I didn't think that being in jail that he would try to take it this far. After months and months of me asking Nigel how he was feeling about you, trying to get him to talk to me, he never wanted to talk about it. So now he writes me a 4 page letter about how he has been feeling. He also wrote about some other things other than you that he is unhappy about. First let me go back and explain, because I never told you this. When Nigel was transferred from Smyrna to Georgetown, he didn't want to go. He's reasons for not wanting to be transferred was because he thought that Lionel Williamson was in that prison. Now I know that DOC does what they want to do; you have no say, this I understand. They have their rules, regulations and policies. However, Nigel knowing or not knowing this, expressed to the prison that he didn't want to be transferred and why. Hear DOC tell it, everything about your case as far as those that are locked up that were charged in your case are supposed to be away or out of the general area of Nigel, so there's is no contact, so they say. Nigel just doesn't want to take any chances of passing by these guys in anyway. I totally understand that, I know exactly where Nigel is coming from. So because the CO's are only following orders, they got to do what they got to do, and they got to pack Nigel up and transfer him to Georgetown. Nigel puts up a fight, I don't know all that happen, but as a result of what he did while being transferred, they charged him with attempted escape, even though he wasn't trying to escape, he just didn't want to go to Georgetown and be around any of those other boys, so they put him in solitary confinement for 90 days. This was back in April, I think. Anyway, Nigel has nothing to do in there but sit and think about everything, so....abracadabra...out comes this letter. He tells me that he has talked to some other blood gang members in the prison he met, and asked them for their protection and to help him fight, because he wants to go after ANYBODY that is friends with the 3 guys that took you away. He not only wants to go after the 3 boys, but their friends too. Marcus, those boys Lionel Williamson, Kurt Dupree and Warren Brooks are also supposed to be blood gang members too. He did not give me the names of these guys who he allegedly hooked up with in prison, but they want $20 a month from him to do this. He said there are two of them. Nigel is getting himself into something dangerous! These boys don't care nothing about him. For one, they want money, they probably don't have anyone on the outside helping them out, and second, what makes Nigel think that these guy are going to fight their own blood members? This shit is crazy. Evidently, a person in the cell next to him is supposedly the head, the top, a master or whatever they call themselves of the bloods in Delaware. And everybody does or is supposed to do what he says. Nigel is in over his head! If anything they just might spread the word around about what Nigel is doing or who he's after. Marcus, you know what Nigel said to me. After all the BS that I have gone through with you, Nigel says to me that he is ready to die to bring you back. He also said that he thinks that you would want him to do this for you. Marcus I am so scared for Nigel right now, He is still locked up in solitary right now, so he's alright, but if this is what's been on his mind all this time, I don't know what is going to happen when he gets out and back into general population. I knew that sitting in solitary would not be good for him with all that has been happening to him. I knew that he had pain in his heart and it's just been festering. I feel that if he had not gone into solitary, if they had not transferred him to Georgetown that he would be doing something to keep his mind off of it, like working in the kitchen, or in some other type of program. Nigel said to me that he is going to catch another charge. Marcus, what am I going to do? I feel so helpless. I wish that there was something I could do for him to take his pain away. You and him were so close. I can't lose Nigel too. And I know that it's just Nigel's pain talking to him, and on the outside, I could get him help, he is still young, he has never experienced death before, this is new to him. But I understand and feel almost the same as him as far as wanting revenge.The prison counselors don't have any real concern or compassion for what inmates go through. And Nigel is a lot like me in that aspect, kind-of, he doesn't talk, he doesn't really share his emotions or feelings. In his letter he said that the jail is taking a toll on him mentally and emotionally. He said that it feels like his mind is racing 100 mph and that he feels so angry all the time about what happened to you. I know that his feelings are real, he describes them perfectly, and I know exactly what he is feeling. Those are real feelings that he is having. He has not gone through anything like this before so I know that what he is saying is real, 'cause I feel it coming through his letter! He says a lot in his letter and I can feel his pain just by reading it. I don't know what to do! I think, well I know that Nigel is crying out for help, and I or no one can, will help him. What do I do? Do you know what this would do to me if something happened to Nigel? Marcus what am I going to do? I feel so bad for Nigel,but at the same time, I can truly relate to how he is feeling, because I want revenge too!

Nigel deep down is such a great kid, just like you. He is so charming, and has such an infectious smile.

## Saturday, July 13, 2013 @ 9:25 PM

I was just thinking about your court case. Why is it that you are my child, a crime was committed against you, which in turn was also committed against me, but I had no say as to the punishment? The lawyers basically advised me as to what was being done or how things are going to happen. I know that they have to follow the book, but not once did they ask me what I would like to see done. I think that the victims' family should have some influence on the outcome of the punishment, even if what we want is only taken under consideration, if you know what I'm trying to say.

Nigel wrote me another letter. He sounded much better in this letter. He didn't talk about you too much this time. He basically just talked about other things. But he did say that he is scared, not just for himself, but for those other people too because of what he might do if he sees them. I can't blame him. I hope he can find another way to channel his emotions. Your friend Holly told me today that she got a letter from him, and she said that his tone sounded like he was in a dark place. I'm glad she wrote to him. Not to many people are writing to him, but that is how people are, they are in your face when you out on the street, talking about give me, give me, give me, then you don't hear from them at all when you locked down. Don't worry Nigel, I got you, LOL. I 'm not a writer, but I am going to try to write to him more, and talk to you more too.

## Wednesday, July 24, 2013 @ 10:55 PM

Some mornings Marcus, I just don't want to get up out of bed. I can't except that you are not here. It's still like a dream for me. It's been 21 months now, and it still feels like I just talked to you yesterday. I feel like it was just yesterday when I saw your car parked outside in the parking lot. I can't think about you without crying. I miss you so much. I would give up every ambition and every desire to have you back. I don't go out to see you all that much, it hurts too much knowing that your there in that place. I feel so alone. I want you home, here with me. Sometimes my stomach hurts so much that I could just throw up. I get these knots in the middle of chest, and I can actually feel myself trying to push the knot down. Every time I ride past the Sunoco Gas Station, I get that knot in my chest. I try to sing, I try to play the music loud, it helps a little, but not much, because I still have to think about what I'm doing and why I'm doing it. What I say to myself, it's like..."ok, I'm about to cry, I'm thinking about Marcus again and it's hurting me, let me turn up the music, let me think about the words to this song in an effort to try not to think about it as I'm driving past this gas station." I have to make a conscious effort to do that. But it's a pointless effort, it still hurts.

## Monday, July 29, 2013 @ 5:05 PM

Today I was thinking about all the things I wanted to do with you and Nigel as a family, all the things that I should have done with the two of you when y'all were younger. With you being gone, it makes me think about the "could-of, should-of's." I wish I had taken the both of you to amusements parks more often like Great Adventure or Bush Gardens. I wish I could go back in time and do something's over again. Right now, I think about how much Nigel might be blaming himself for what happen to you. My heart hurts for him so much. I miss you both so much. You know I still feel like I am alone with my feelings. Everybody else has moved on, can't say that I blame them, because it hurts to be where I am, stuck. I wouldn't wish this on anyone. So many times I wish that I could hear your voice, just to hear you say "Mom" just one more time. Nobody calls me anymore to see how I am doing. Well I wouldn't say nobody, Jamere, Milan, Rashandra, Will; they do call me from time to time. But at the same time, I don't mind, 'cause it's just a reminder of you. There was a point when I enjoyed people calling me asking or checking to see if I'm ok, but not so much now, so it does and it doesn't bother me when people call.

You and Nigel were more than just my kids, we had a good relationship, I enjoyed you guys. Nigel always the joker, you always the instigator. But it's still hard to pull myself back up from this whole situation. There are still many days when I just want to give up. But I have Nigel, he is saving my life right now. I know you might or people might think that I should be past this stage of emotions right now. But, some days Marcus, I just don't know. I laugh, talk and go about my day as if nothing is wrong, when deep inside I am so broken. I can't explain how easy it would be for me right now to end this. I'm just not happy. Marcus, I am not happy! I don't know how else to say it, it's just how I feel. You would think that my 12 year relationship with Garry, that I should be happy, and it's not him, believe me, but I'm not happy. What I'm feeling, the sadness that I can't let go of goes beyond him, it's separate from him. It's you and Nigel, it's you! You are my child, my blood, a part of me is gone. I can't never get that back. I can't talk, laugh, hug, touch you ever again. To know that you can and will NEVER be able to have something, specifically someone ever again is powerful. I want so badly just to yell at you about something, about nothing, and I can't.

I'm sitting out here to Silver Lake again, and there are these 3 little girls walking by with their mother, I look at them and I imagine if one of them could be your daughter. I know that for years I told you and Nigel not to make me a grandmother, I would give the both of you condoms to make sure of that, I always told you to protect yourself, but now, but now, I wish!!! Sometimes I daze at little girls and just wonder if you do have any kids out there that you didn't want to tell me about. If so, I wish they would find me.

I'm back home from the park now, I'm just sitting here in the driveway, I don't want to go in the house, it's just more of the same.

## Wednesday, July 31, 2013 @ 1:15 AM

I wish you would respond or say something about some of the things I've been talking to you about, because now I have these feeling that I want to write Lionel Williamson a letter. I'm not ready and don't want to see him face-to-face, I just want to ask him what was the real reason why he did this. Because I don't believe that bull shit statement in court about some damn argument that happen a year prior, and car chases, other people getting shot. And why wasn't anything that he was claiming reported to the police. I guess when your not living right, you avoid the police. I really, really want to know why that girl Emily's name was brought up. What did she have to do with any of this. Because I always thought from the begining that she had something to do with it. It was even being said that she was cheating on you with Lionel Williamson. I want to hear the truth. You are not here to defend yourself. I also want to ask him where the gun is, what did he do with it? I need to show and tell him how I've been doing, how much this is hurting me.

## Saturday, August 3, 2013 @1:15 PM

Hey Marcus, I'm lying here in bed; I'm thinking back on how much I miss those sounds from the neighbors in the apartment upstairs walking around at all hours of the night, it sometimes sounded like you were walking in the house. I remember how I couldn't sleep at night, because the sounds would make me scared. Even though it made me restless, I want it back, because I don't feel your presence anymore in the new house. Every night it was like I slept with one eye open and one eye closed, waiting. If I did fall asleep, it was a light sleep, because as soon as I would hear the least little bit of noise, I would be looking out the bed room door, I always slept with my door open, I wanted to see you walk by. But oddly enough, those sounds and wanting you to walk in, made me a nervous wreck, but now that I'm in the new house, I would give anything to hear it again. I told you before that the last couple of days in the old apartment I didn't want to move anymore, because I was feeling like I was leaving you behind. And now I don't have anything! No sounds, no nothing. Does this mean that I am forgetting you, are you leaving me now? I don't want you to go Marcus. I remember that night in the apartment when I was sleeping, and I felt your presence sit down on the foot of bed next to my feet, I felt the pressure or something heavy push the bed down, like it would if someone sat down next to me, it was so real. I woke up and looked down at the bed, but you weren't there. But yet I felt you, I just knew it was you that sat down next to me. And now, I haven't even dreamed about you in a while. The last dream I had, we all were at the water park having fun. But I think about you every day. I've been carrying your wallet with me all the time in my purse; it goes everywhere I go, every day. Just to have something of yours on me, with me at all times! I wish I could have found that necklace that you always wore, the black twisted rope with that metal round piece on it, and you had one that had a little cross on it, I know that you probably had one of them on that night, but much like your cell phone, it disappeared too.

## Thursday, August 8, 2013 @ 2:25 AM

Hey Marcus, it's been a while since I've been up at this hour; I guess I have a lot on my mind. How have you been? I miss you so much. I think about you every day. I might not write to you every day, but there is not a day that goes by that I'm not talking to you in my heart. Let's see... what's first, what's been going on in the life of your dear old mom. Yesterday I was talking to an old friend that I kind-of grew up with in Capital Park, I have not seen her in years, since we were preteens. Why people feel that they still need to give me information about something that they know nothing about is beyond me. I guess people want to feel that they are a part of something bigger than themselves. Anyway, she told me that the night of your accident she was living in the same housing park as Lionel Williamson and Warren Brooks, and the house that Lionel Williamson was living in at that time just recently got torn down. She said that the house had the word "killer" spray painted all over it. I don't know how much of that is true, but that's what she told me. Not sure how I feel about that, honestly, don't really care! Tell me what you think about this, I mean tell me if you are ok with me doing this, but I kind-of want to reach out to Lionel Williamson and ask him why? I feel like I need to know more about why he did what he did. I don't want to see him face-to-face; I was going to write him a letter. That is if I'm allowed to do that. I mean now, I just feel he can tell me and say whatever he wants, preferably the truth, no lawyers, no attorneys, no risk or worry about his sentencing. Just him and I talking it out. My heart, my mind won't rest about this. I still need to know. It's not that I'm trying to get into your business, well yes I am, you know I'm nosey like that, LOL. It's just that from what I know about your friends, and the type of people you brought around me, you didn't hang around people like him. I want to know what type of problems he had with you. I just don't believe that bull shit story they gave in court. My heart tells me that there is still something else or someone else behind it all. But I could be wrong, I just want to ask him myself. How do you feel about me doing that?

I have been feeling better or at the least managing my emotions better. I'm trying to redirect my frustrations and anger towards other things, but in a good way. Like your brother, I don't want him to feel that I'm not there for him, so I have been trying to do better with writing to him, and trying to do things for him. I've been focused on your foundation. You know the Conflict Resolution Education class starts in a few weeks. We are going to be at a school in Dover. We have been working with the principal on bringing the program into the school Mon-Thurs. for an hour.

I had lunch with Diane Glenn today. I really enjoy meeting up with her and just talking. You and Nigel always said that I need to get out of the house more, that I'm boring. She asked me how I was and if I'm settled into the new house. I told her yes, somewhat. I said that I don't feel your presence anymore. I always felt in my core that I was leaving you behind, back in Wilmington. Remember I told you that those last couple of days I didn't want to move anymore, because I felt like that was going to happen... remember? And so it did! But I will say this, lately, these past few weeks; I have been feeling like you have been trying to find your way here. It's strange, but every time I hear an unexplainable bump or noise in the house, I have been telling myself that it's just you trying to find your way away around the house. The house is new to you, and you don't know your way around, so your bumping into walls. Garry says it's just the sounds that the house makes when it settles, or the neighbor next door might be moving furniture or hanging pictures or something like that. Well I don't care what anybody says, I know it's you! This is my story and I'm sticking to it, LOL. I just said LOL, Nigel told me not to ever say that again, because I'm not young and hip anymore, little does he know.

I found a picture of you and Nigel at Grandmom's house the other day. You had to be around 6 and Nigel 4. I love this picture so much! Y'all two were great kids at that age. The two of you have the best smiles ever!

You can see the closeness even back then that the two of you had. I love it! This is such a great picture of the two of you at that age. Love it, love it, love it! I wish you had not stopped wanting to get your picture taken. The older you got the more you didn't want your picture taken, or at least for me you didn't. Why is that, because you are truly handsome?

I'm still logging into your Facebook page being nosy. People don't post on your page as much as they used to anymore, People move on, people forget. I know that everybody has their own life, and they shouldn't be stuck and not letting you go like I am. It's just that I need/want to know that people still think about you and love you, and that they miss you just as much as I do. It's like I need validation from others that you existed, I mean yes, you are my son, I gave birth to you, you are more real to me than to anybody, but I still need that confirmation that…..something, telling me that you were loved. I like going on to your Face Book page and seeing that someone posted that they miss you on it. But I'm thinking that I'm going to take your page down, close your FB account a couple of days after your 2nd year mark, maybe!

Well, it's about 3:10 in the morning now; we'll talk again soon, real soon. Because I'm thinking about doing something that I hope you will be ok with. But we'll see, I got to think some more on it first. Going to bed now, love you.

## Thursday, August 13, 2013 @ 1:05 AM

You know Marc, off and on for the past year and a half or so, I keep waking up between the hours of 2 a.m. and 4:30 a.m. I know that it's because my body is still consumed by the trauma of you being killed and the timing of it all, with it being that early in the morning, 4 A.M., this just might be how my body is responding or identifying with the pain. But this morning I am waking up damn mad, I am so angry. Something just came over me from out of no where. When your trial was over, people were saying to me "well, now you can have some closure." WTF! Where does that come from, how do people have the gall to say something like that to people when they don't know what that person is going through? I hate for people to try to inflect on me what they think closure is or should come from, or when it should happen. I hate that! Who are they to tell me that I have closure? You are my son, my child, my blood. You are a part of me that is missing....gone! How do I find closure in that? Your killer is still breathing and walking this earth, in 20 to 30 years when he is released you will still be gone. Closure....really? I don't think so!

## Saturday, August 17, 2013 @ 9:45 AM

I dreamed about you again last night. Garry and I were finally getting married. About 4 or 5 days before the wedding, I kept having moments, emotional moments about you not being there. And every day it got worst. We were getting married at the house; we were having a small house wedding, but a big reception. The day of the wedding I just couldn't go through with the wedding. I wouldn't come out the room. One of your friends was trying to console me, (can't remember who it was) A friend of mine name Tuesday was also trying to help console me too. I just kept crying and crying. I wanted you there so badly. Remember a few years back I told you and Nigel that when I got married that I wasn't going to have any brides maids, that I wanted to have you and Nigel walk for me (not as groomsmen), but instead of having 4 or 5 bride's maids walking down the ales, it would be just you and Nigel, and Garry would probably have his best man and maybe one groomsman. Well, I wanted it something like that. You and Nigel would stand on my side behind me, and when the officiant would say "who gives this woman to be married to this man?" You and Nigel would both say: "We Do." Y'all would be my bro-maids, LOL, But the day of the wedding, I just couldn't go through with it. It meant so much for me to have both my sons at my wedding to give me away. But now, I think that what I'll do is in addition to lighting the unity candle with Garry, that I will also light another candle that represents you being there, we will light them separately, yours first! Dad's not here to give me away, and the order should fall to the eldest brother to give me away. Not that I wouldn't mind having Butchy give me away, it was just always my dream that if it wasn't dad, that it would be you and Nigel.

**Friday, August 30, 2013 @ 9:40 PM**

Hey Marcus, it's been a long week! As you know I started back to school at Del Tech. I'm making my second attempt at a Human Services Degree. It got me to remembering and thinking back, one weekend when you came home from work, you told me that you wanted to go to college. I looked at you like "yeah right," I said "ok, it must be some girl you met", you just smiled. Don't laugh...I know you remember! You were asking me all these different questions about financial aid, and what I think you should major in. It was only months later when I could see that you were actually serious, because you kept asking and talking to me about it. Even a few months before you passed we were talking about you taking classes at Del Tech in Wilmington. You know, it would have been nice to see you go away to school and do something different. That's really one of the things that I liked about the job that you had, you were able to see, go and do different things. It took you to different places and states, even though you were only home on the weekends, you were out being a man, making your own money. But at the same time I know that you were tired of it. You got the job when you were 18, and worked it for 3 ½ years. You were not able to do things that young adults your age do in their early 20's. So I understood your frustration about that. I just really wish you had been able to experience college life.


**Sunday, September 1, 2013 @ 7:45 PM**

Hey Marcus, there is this guy on Facebook, you might know him. His name is Conrad Jones, his Facebook name is Big Baby Jones, he made this music rap video of a few people who died in Dover, or at least I think that they are all from Dover. Well, the video is made to be like a remembrance, a tribute to those that died to violence. He raps about people who died and how much they are missed. He mentioned you in it as "Smiley", right at the point that he mentioned your name, your picture popped up. He has pictures flashing of all the people who died in it. I thought that it was very nice, a very well done video. It can be very emotional if you know a lot of the people that's in it. And most of them seem to be just kids, I mean they all look like they are in their early 20's, no older than 30. It's just sad! I think Nikki said that it's also on YouTube called R.I.P. – Baby Corleone (Honorable Mention Mix) or something like that. When you get a chance look at it, I know you are going to like it. You're probably with most of them now. I know that you liked your rap music, but Nigel was the Rapper between the two of you. I remember that I was always yelling at you to turn your music down. Oh, and Pull Your Pants Up! LOL, stop laughing, I know you remember! I miss you so much. It's amazing how those little petty things that I use to scream and yell at you about seem so funny now.

**Thursday, September 5, 2013 @ 9:10 PM**

Marcus I rode past the Sunoco gas station today, and there was this situation similar to yours, whereas there were two cars parked on the North side of the gas station and one car parked on the South end facing away from the highway, facing towards the Home Depot store. I started having flashes in my head if this is how your car was situated that night. I didn't look at the surveillance video from the gas station of that night, but from the way that Sgt. Spicer explained or described it to me, your car was on the N. bound side of the gas station facing

North, and the car that Lionel Williamson, Kurt Dupree, and Warren Brooks were in, was on the S. bound side of the gas station. There were a couple of cars parked next to you one of which was going to give you a jump start. Anyway, something came over me, something like a white haze covered my eyes, all I could think about was you, and snap shots and images of what my mind pieced together of what happened to you or how that whole situation went down or played out just came over me. I wanted to drive over there to the gas station and tell them that they should leave, that it's not safe for them to be here. I just wanted those people to leave.

It also made me think back on another time when I was in Wawa at the register paying for some gum or something; I caught myself staring out the window. The parking lot was full of young people hanging out talking and getting gas. I felt myself in this deep stare looking, hoping that I would see you. I just knew that I was going to see you out there joking and talking to your friends. I felt myself doing this, when I pulled myself out of it, the lady at the register asked me if I was ok, a couple of people just walked around me because I was just standing there, she said that I looked like I was about to cry, that was embarrassing! I miss you so much Marcus. Even though I'm doing better, it still feels unreal, I just talked to you. Apart of me still won't, can't accept that your gone.

I went to go see Nigel yesterday, remember how I could be looking right at you and be calling you Nigel, or him Marcus? Yesterday Nigel said, stop calling me Marcus, he laughed about it but I know that it bothers him. It's just something that all mothers do, call their children by another child's name. My mom called me Nikki or Dawn all the time.

Well, I don't know how he does it, but Warren Brooks is out of jail again. The VINE system said he got on bail. I just don't get it! How is he always getting out? I thought for sure, this time he was going to be in jail for a good long time. Sgt Spicer or anyone can't tell me what's going on with him because these charges have nothing to do with your case. They already got off with a slap on the hand with your case. It's just not fair!

I do have some good news for you. Don't get excited! But your foundations Youth Conflict Resolution class starts on Monday, September 9th, I am so excited. I think this program can really do the young kids some good. These are going to be good lessons learned. No one needs to end up in your or my situation ever again. The Dover Post is doing a short article about it. They called today and talked with Garry and me, asking us questions. They are going to meet us at the school on Monday to take pictures. How you likin' that? I've asked Mayor Carey and Dave Spicer if they would be there. You know I had to ask Dave, he's important to me. But I can't wait, this is going to be a good thing for the kids.

**Saturday, Sept 7, 2013 @ 10:05 AM**

I've got two things to tell you today Marcus. First thing, I didn't have a very good evening or night last night. But I'm going to tell you about my dream first because I don't want to forget it. Ok, I'm not sure how it began, but I remember we had a family day with you at the cemetery. Now for some reason your head stone was different, it was one of those big square, block headstones, instead of the one you have right now, which is flat and flush with the ground. Now your head stone was down low for some reason. You know how when you go to the zoo and animals are in a pit, like the lions pit, you got to look down over a fence or railing to see them, that's the best way for me to describe it to you. That's what I remember, looking over a rail and down at your headstone. When we looked around the cemetery, everything else was normal, it looked like a regular cemetery, yours was the only one that appeared that we had to look down into a hole at. I can remember Nikki, Talia and someone else being there with me. Now we were looking around at some of the other head stones that were real fancy, some were marble, some had pictures, but yours was this real nice gray stone, shiny marble, it was just square and big, but yours also had a big straight through hole in it, like if I wanted to put a candle or ornaments in the middle of your headstone or something like that. It's weird, because we were standing over so high above your headstone, we could only see the flat top of it, but yet, we could see just a little of the hole, but you can only see the hole if you are in front or on an angle of it. (Dreams, go figure!)

Anyway, we noticed that some of the headstones that we were looking at had little stuffed fluffy toy cats built into them, half-and-half, like fancy decorations. Half of the body you couldn't see, but the head and two front paws where sticking out. Sounds crazy but stay with me Marc, I'm trying to paint the picture for you. I guess they were for cat lovers. Anyway, Talia and I was looking over the rail at your head stone, and she stared sharing her cookie with you. She would toss them into the hole that was in your headstone, Marcus this is a dream, crazy things happen in dreams, LOL. So she was tossing cookies into the hole of your headstone right, now we are looking down on your headstone, we could not see your headstone from the front, just from the top, remember?

But yet, for some reason I could see the hole, a little bit! So, Talia tossed her cookie in the whole, and a few seconds later, this hand, this arm came out real quick and tossed the cookie on the ground. It happened so fast! Nikki and I looked at each other without words as if to say, "did you see that?" So Talia tossed another cookie in the hole, and again a few seconds later a hand and arm came out real fast and dropped to cookie on the ground again. I started screaming! I don't know if I started screaming because I saw your arm or because you didn't want the cookie, or if someone was playing a bad joke on me. (Remember we can't see completely into the hole, because we are looking down, from over top of your headstone) About this time your Uncle Butch gets there, someone tossed another cookie, except this time it took a little longer before you tossed it back out on the ground. Marcus, I was freaking out, I was screaming and yelling for you to come out. Was someone playing a joke on me, was there a little kid hiding in the hole of your headstone? Over and over you kept throwing the cookies out. I can remember that I was so frantic that I passed out. And that is when I woke up. Apart of me thinks that you just wanted me to know that you were there. Because normally when I'm visiting with you and fixing up, cleaning up your area, the wind will blow, even on days when the wind wasn't blowing, I know that's your way of telling me that your there with me. But don't do that Marcus, I can't take that, my heart is still hurting, even now that I'm awake talking to you, it hurts. It just made me remember how back at the apartment in Wilmington, you were always trying to scare me. Sneaking into my room in the dark, hiding behind doors, but you never could scare me, but you got me this time.

Ok, now, got the dream out the way. The other thing I wanted to tell you happen yesterday afternoon.

Marcus, I am so angry, mad, upset, disappointed, pissed off, frustrated, outraged! The school where we WERE supposed to start the Youth Conflict Resolution classes on Monday, (the day after tomorrow) called me at 4:55 p.m. (Yesterday, Friday, at damn near 5pm) to tell me that they have to put our program on hold. What the hell! It's Friday, the program starts on Monday, really! We have been planning this since last year! They said that the school board has been cracking down and scrutinizing the different programs that have been coming into the schools. How do they just now tell me this with just 2 days to go that this is happening? The Dover Post was doing an article on us about the program; they wanted us to be over to the school to take pictures on Monday. The Mayor was going to be there, Sgt. Spicer was going to be there. Marc, this is not my fault. They could have told me this a long time ago, earlier in the year, over the summer, or last year, not 2 days before the program begins! They said that it has to be reviewed and approved by the school board. Their exact words were "we have to put the program on HOLD for now," but gave no indication as to how long it may be on hold. Marcus, as many face-to-face meetings that we had with the school talking about the program, if there was anything we needed to know about the school board needing to review our curriculum, they had PLENTY of time to tell us, actually, the school gave us the ok for the program, if it was a school board issue, you would think that they would have or did take care of that already, or at the least earlier in our meetings, you would think that they would have given us the heads up about the school board. They could have told us that before we can proceed with the program that x, y, and z issues needs to be done first. But noooo! This is just crazy! Come Monday morning, I got to call the Mayor and Dover Post and tell them not to come, I got to call Dave and tell him not to come. I got to call the school and get more information as to what is going on. I mean, they only called me at 5:00 on Friday late afternoon, nothing I can do until Monday. Marcus we came so close, and now the rug is pulled out from under us! We were only 2 days away. I was so frustrated and irritated Friday night, I started getting sick, I mean, I started getting woozy and light headed, my stomach started turning, the feeling just came over me quick. I had to shut it down, I went to bed around 8:00, this is why I didn't tell you any of this last night, my head just starting hurting so bad. This is just so unbelievable!

## Sunday, September 8, 2013 @ 9:45 PM

Hey, I'm not going to be long. It's exactly one month away today from the 2 year mark since you've been gone. It's still unreal. It's still hard to swallow that your gone. Sometimes when I think about you, it's like I just talked to you. I miss you so much. I'll be calling the school first thing in the morning. I'll let you know what happens.

## Monday, September 9, 2013 @ 10:30 PM

THERE'S GOING TO BE NO PROGRAM AT THIS SCHOOL! Marc I am so disappointed, I can't even explain. Marcus I wanted so badly for your program to be a success. I honestly have no words for what just happen. Well, I will say that there is still going to be a program, somewhere, just not with that school. So, Garry and I called this morning to get more clarification as to what is going on. At first he says the same thing that he left on my voice mailbox, that the school board needed to review the program. But when we started talking about the mayor being a supporter of the program, and people's job being on the line and other people who support our program, he says, ok, well, let me make a couple of phone calls and get back with you. Garry told him that we really need to know something by 3 p.m. because we have a lot on the line with this. He calls back with not much better news. He says that they still want the program, but because other organizations are trying to bring programs into the school, he has to change what he originally agreed to. He wants to give us 1-day a week on Thursdays for 45 min. WTF, Really! I don't mean to be ungrateful, but we went from planning for the past 8 or 9 months to have this program 4-days a week, Mon–Thurs., for an hour. That is how the curriculum is written. We won't make any real impact on these kids with a one day a week class. We can't get any real measurable results with one day a week! That's like setting us up to fail. I mean, I know that any help a child can get is needed, and it's all about them, it's just not realistic for us. Oh, also as part of the one day arrangement that the school wanted to give us, they also said they don't want for us to have a press/news release about the program or the news article that the paper was going to do on us. They don't want the press taking pictures because kids might be in the pictures and parents might have a problem with that. Now that I can understand, but we could have taken pictures in front of the school with the school officials that helped us with the program, us, the Mayor and Sgt. Spicer. Kids didn't have to be in the picture at all. So I called the Mayor and told him the situation and I talked to Sgt. Spicer, he understood. Dave is so accommodating. And I know that I am asking these people for favors and I don't want them to start saying "oh, it's Joreen; here she comes again wanting something else." And I know that this situation was out of my control, but I feel like it makes me look incompetent. I try not to ask for too many things of people, after a while it gets old. And what about Ashley, the instructor we hired? We have been dragging her along with us on this for about 5 months now; she's depending on this, on us, for a job. And now she has nothing. She could have found something more full time, closer to where she lives. She needed this job. I'm mad at us for her. We should have had a backup plan; I just didn't see this coming. I didn't think that we would have needed a backup plan, I mean; we have been working on this project for months with the school. They should have told us long ago. I feel like such a failure. So needless to say, we called the school and told them that one day a week just was not going to work for us, back to the drawing board.

## Thursday, September 19, 2013 @ 10:15 PM

Hey Marcus, I wish you could tell me what I should do about forgiveness. I keep hearing this forgiveness will give me peace. But I just don't think that I can. No matter if I decide to forgive, you will still be gone. I will still be without you, how do I find forgiveness in that. How do I forgive the person that took my son's life, if anything, it will give Lionel Williamson peace not me. It gives him peace knowing that the mother of the person that he killed forgives him for killing her son, Hell NO! I can't do that. How does Nigel find forgiveness in being an only child now? People talk about forgiveness as if you can take some magic pill and poof, everything will be better, and I'll find closure. I hate it when people say that! And that always seems to come from people who haven't experienced this type of loss. They even said that after the trial was over, that now I'll be able to find closure, NO! I haven't found anything, closure or forgiveness. This is my private hell that I'm living in, you know nothing about what I am going through. Then someone said to me that when my heart is ready to forgive that it will just come to me. I just don't know Marc. All I know is that sometimes I feel like a prisoner. I don't go to the mall, and not just because I don't have any money. I mean, I just don't want to be confronted, I don't want to be around a lot of people. I don't want people asking me how I'm doing, or looking at me any type of way. And I especially don't want to be in any area where the other families might be. Dover is small, they could be right next to me, and I wouldn't know it. I feel that they know who I am, that they know what I look like, but I don't them. I sometimes feel like I'm being watched by them and it makes me not want to go anywhere, especially by myself. I don't like the uncertainty of being out in public, out in the open, especially when I'm by myself. Sometimes when I go to Walmart in Camden, I'm in and out with the quickness. I know exactly what I am going in there for and where it's at, I go straight there; I don't spend any time looking around at other things, walking through the isles, none of that! I just feel so much better in my own surroundings. I guess some might call this being a prisoner in my own skin, but that's ok, because this is where I feel safe. But it's not the type of safe where I feel like I'm in danger, but more about knowing that I won't have to run into people that I don't want to be around, specifically the other boys families. And too, I don't even like going to the Walmart in Camden, because the other boys' families are from around that area. I think that I would be likely to run into them in the Camden Walmart then in the one in Dover. But still you never know. So, if always being home and staying in the house gives me comfort, then so be it.

## Wednesday, September 18, 2013 @ 8:15 PM

Nigel just called me tonight. He said that he went through his first hearing phase for his interstate compact transfer, and they did recommend him for transfer. He said that he has 2 more phases to go through before they give the final approval. He told me that he expressed to them that he wanted to be moved to an outer state prison to eliminate any possibilities of meeting up with those boys or any of their associates. He said something about the prison does or did a survey and it showed that there are blood gang members in all 3 Delaware prisons. I know that he is relieved that the first phase recommended him for a transfer and so am I. He is hoping that they send him to PA. It will mean a longer ride for me to visit with him, but at least he won't be in that situation anymore. You and I both know that Nigel ain't no punk, but if this makes him more comfortable, then so be it. And I don't want Nigel getting into any more trouble because he done jacked somebody up.

## Thursday, September 26, 2013 @ 9:50 PM

I feel bad Marcus. Today, tonight was the "Day of Remembrance" for murdered victims event in Wilmington, I didn't go. For two reasons, one, because I had class, we have a lot of assignments that's due and I need to focus. And two, I didn't feel like being sad. I didn't want to be emotional, and I know that's what would have happen had I gone. I would have seen your picture go across the screen; I just would have fallen apart. Plus with everyone else there crying and feeling sad, that's just too much emotion for me. I just didn't go, just thinking about it makes me sad.

## Tuesday, October 8, 2013 @ 3:50 AM

I should have seen this coming, up….at this hour….again,
Wow!!

Hey Marcus, today is your 2 year mark that you've been
gone. Someone the other day said to me that "in a couple
of days it will be your son's two year anniversary of his
death." I had to stop and correct them. I told them that
an anniversary is something that is celebrated; I wish
not to celebrate the date of my son's death! I choose to
call it your/the "mark" of your death. You might have
also noticed that all this time that I have been writing
and talking to you about 'them boys' that I have always
referred to them by their full name. I not once referred to
them by just their first name. I just feel that calling them
by just their first name is me giving them…something. I
don't know, I just don't feel right or just don't want to call
them by just their first name. It almost makes me feel like
I have a personal relationship or connection with them,
like we're friends. You don't call people that you just met
or really don't know all that well by their first names do
you? No, you call them Mr. or Ms. so-n-so, why should I
give them that honor. So I just call them by their full name.
It's almost like me calling them by their first name is me
validating of acknowledging their existence, and I care
not for who they are!  It's hard to explain what I mean.

I still have not gotten up the courage to go to the gas
station yet, not sure if I ever will. But still, there is a
part of me that just wants to walk your last steps, and
feel your pain. I want to be where you were that last
day. I don't know, it's like I need to feel your presence
there. I still want to talk to the EMS that transported you
to the hospital; I want to know if you said anything, if

you called for me, if you knew what had just happen, if you were in any pain, so many unanswered questions.

I still don't have all the answers as to why this happen to you; I guess I'll never get them. The only person who can give them to me is Lionel Williamson, and that's if he has really accepted what he did and is willing to be 100% truthful with me, which I think is highly unlikely. I'm still asking myself if I want to meet with him to talk about why he did this, or at the least, write him a letter telling him how what he did has ruined my life

So many days, I still feel like I just want to die, trying to except that you are no longer here is sooo hard. I just didn't want to go on without you, you and Nigel are my life. There is nothing about having the two of you that I would take back. There are days when thinking about you makes it so hard to just breathe sometimes. But, something kept me here, it was Nigel! I know that he is missing you just as much as I am.


## Tuesday, October 8, 2013 @ 9:55 PM

Nigel called me earlier tonight. I think he knew that I was feeling sad today. He joked with me about putting his foot down with me when he gets home, and that I'm not going to be smothering him, by asking him 50 questions about where he is, what he's doing, and who he's with. I told him that if it were not for me, he wouldn't be in this world, and he will do what I say for as long as I say. We just kept going back and forth like that; he brought a smile to my face. I told him that he's still a momma's boy.

You know Marcus, I told you about how angry I was

with my family and some of your friends, and how I didn't think that they cared enough because they didn't support me/us. Well maybe I was wrong for that. I mean this is my problem, my issues, I can't blame them for not understanding or expect anything from them. Maybe I was asking for too much from them. It was just how I felt at the time, I can't expect them to understand how it feels or what it's like to lose a child. And for that I am sorry, I don't want you to think that they don't care about you.

Marcus a lot of your friends represented you on Facebook today, more than I had expected, but there were some that I did expect to post something that didn't, but that's ok. It was just good to see that people still love you. Every day I look at your pictures, and I just can't seem to stay off of your FB page, it's just so unreal!

Marcus, I cannot begin to tell you how much loosing you has left a hole in my heart, my heart has such a big void, and I don't know how to fill it. That knock on the door at 4 AM on October 8, 2011 has changed me forever, it's been the darkest day of my life. I miss you, Nigel misses you. But if there is one thing that gives me solace, is knowing that our last words to each other on the last day that we talked, was I love you. And Marcus, I do love you.

05/12/2006

www.ingramcontent.com/pod-product-compliance
Lightning Source LLC
Chambersburg PA
CBHW072058090426
42739CB00012B/2803